D0205541

A GUIDE TO
LITERARY
STUDY

Leon T. Dickinson

IN THIS SERIES

A GUIDE TO LITERARY STUDY

LEON T. DICKINSON

University of Missouri

HOLT, RINEHART AND WINSTON

New York   Chicago   San Francisco

Toronto   London

ISBN 0-03-008270-6

123   008   232221

FOREWORD

This book is designed to help college students get their bearings in elementary courses in literature. Part One considers the several ways to approach literary study (Chapter I). It also discusses the major forms of imaginative literature and the basic techniques of these forms (Chapters II–IV). Part Two, more immediately practical, makes specific suggestions on how to study literature and how to write about it (Chapters V, VI). Because these several matters are elementary, they are essential. In the college classroom they are sometimes presented systematically, but often, simply because they are elementary, it is assumed that they have been mastered in high school. In either case students should find it helpful to have these ABC's of literary study collected here for ready reference.

In planning the book, I received useful advice from my colleagues at the University of Missouri. Professor William M. Gibson, of New York University, read the manuscript and gave valuable criticism. The book profited also from suggestions of the publisher's staff, notably Professor Richard S. Beal, of Boston University. To all of these friends I am grateful.

L.T.D.

Columbia, Missouri
July, 1959

CONTENTS

PART ONE

• I •

THE NATURE OF
LITERARY STUDY

A student in a college literature course may feel that he is expected to learn many different kinds of things. One class session may be concerned with an author's life; the next with political, social, religious, philosophical, or scientific backgrounds of literature; a third with questions of literary technique. These matters are all interesting and valid areas for study, but their variety is sometimes puzzling. What are the most important things to study? Where to begin? What to emphasize? Usually a teacher explains early in the course what his approach will be and what he considers most important. The possible approaches are several.

APPROACHES TO LITERARY STUDY

1. The Literary Work in Relation to Its Backgrounds

To some extent a literary work is a product of its time and place. Although if a work is good it often reaches beyond those limits and has "universal" qualities, it also springs from a particular age, one that may be quite different from our own. Especially with older literature we must exercise our historical imagination and do what we can to regard a work as nearly as possible in the way its contemporaries regarded it. This means that in addition to using the dictionary, we must acquaint ourselves with what we usually call the "backgrounds" of literature—political developments, social conditions, religious ideas and practices, philosophic concepts —which help us to see a work in its historical and intellectual context. Chaucer's "Nun's Priest's Tale," for instance, contains many references to medieval physiology. We can better understand *Paradise Lost* if we know something of Milton's theological views. We read the *Essays* of Emerson more intelligently when we learn the religious and philosophic concepts that influenced his thinking. Such background material may be treated briefly in one's assigned textbook and may be discussed by the teacher in class. It is often desirable, though, especially in advanced classes, to supplement this information with independent reading.

2. The Literary Work in Relation to the Author

Literary study sometimes involves studying the lives of authors; Samuel Johnson, in fact, found the "biographical part" of literature the most interesting. Biographical study can have several aims: (a) One may study the author's life for itself. (b) One may read the author's works as documents in his biography. (c) Or one may study an author's life for the light it sheds on his writings. The first of these uses of biography presents no problems. Nor does the second, except that one must be careful in drawing inferences about a man from his writings; the "I" in a lyric poem, for instance, cannot always be taken to refer literally to the personality of the poet. As for the third, just how much light can be shed on a literary work by biography is debatable. Often biography can show us how the work came to be written, what went into its making and why, and how the writer worked in the process of creation. Browning's life in Italy and his acquaintance with Renaissance painting show us how he was led to write "Fra Lippo Lippi" and perhaps account for the presence of some details in the poem. But such details do little to help us understand the poem itself. Questions of literary genesis (how the work came into being), of sources (what materials the author used), and of literary craftsmanship (how the author worked) are interesting ones, though they are usually the concern of the advanced student. But however interesting, they should not be regarded as substitutes for questions about the work itself.

3. The Literary Work in Relation to Its Readers

Since we read in order to be instructed, moved, entertained, it is perhaps natural that in talking about a literary work we should speak of how it affects us. Some works in particular seem to invite such comment. We speak of the pity and indignation we feel on reading Steinbeck's *The Grapes of Wrath,* or the enchantment we experience in reading Coleridge's "Kubla Khan." The mere statement of how one feels about a literary work is not very significant literary commentary, although it is a natural and pleasant activity. The personal reaction to a work, however, can be a starting point for further investigation. One may go on and ask *why* he feels the way he does, or what there is in the work that causes his feeling. Although this procedure has its dangers for an inexperienced reader, whose initial response may really be unjustified, it can lead more mature readers to a significant and revealing commentary on the work.

Another way to explore the relation between the literary work and the reader is to inquire into the way the work has been received, that is, what people have thought of it. The plays of Shakespeare were popular in his day and have been admired ever since, though more so in some periods than in others. Herman Melville was all but forgotten in the last thirty years of his life, but has come in our time to be regarded as a truly great writer. To study the course of a writer's reputation and to discover how his works have been regarded in different ages are legitimate ways to examine the work-reader relationship. One should realize, however, that study of this kind, often of interest to advanced students, sheds more light on one part of the relationship than on the other. It tells us more about the readers than about the work.

4. The Literary Work in Relation to Other Literature

Many times our understanding of a particular work of literature may be deepened by seeing its place in literary history, by exploring its relation to other works written at the same time or in the same period, or by comparing it to other works of the same genre. Literary works are written at certain times; they are influenced by earlier works and in turn influence later works; they reflect literary vogues, when a certain type of writing or literary theory or philosophic attitude is popular, and the causes and results of these vogues are discoverable. A chronicle of literary events, which seeks to show not only what happened but why it happened, we call a literary history. In addition to histories covering the entire literary development of a country—the history of English literature, of American literature, for example—we have histories of particular periods (the Romantic period), of particular types at certain periods (the development of Elizabethan drama), or of particular literary vogues (local-color writing in America after the Civil War). Such histories are invaluable as records of literary activity. No special competence, however, is required to study them; from them one acquires facts as one does from a political, military, or constitutional history. They can provide a beginning student with a useful frame into which he can fit what he knows. But one must remember that to "know about" literature is not to know literature.

A second way in which literary works are studied in relation to one another is by considering together the writings of a particular period— the early eighteenth century, the Romantic period, the decade in America following the First World War. Because the works of a given period often have characteristics and qualities in common, one possible procedure is to learn these common characteristics and then to see wherein an individual work exhibits them. The danger here is that one reads with a preconceived notion of what the work ought to be like; instead of trying to see the work for what it is, one may make of reading a mere hunting game—may, for instance, read Keats's odes in order to discover in them "aspects of Romanticism."

Still a third way to study works in relation to one another is to bring into comparison works of a similar genre (poems of similar types, short stories, plays), as is done in introductory "types" courses in literature. The method is valuable because the process of comparison (of two things which can legitimately be compared) is an excellent way to reveal salient features of each individual work.

5. The Literary Work as an Entity in Itself

The approaches to literature discussed so far presuppose familiarity with the literature itself. Their concerns are not necessarily peripheral matters, but they are secondary ones. The first concern always, especially in elementary study, is the literary texts themselves. All of us err in literary study insofar as we direct our attention to secondary matters before we make ourselves familiar at first hand with the writings to which they are related. This principle would seem to be self-evident, but it is not always observed. Elementary students tend to forget it if they by-pass the text in the hope of finding a short cut to literary competence. Advanced students lose sight of it if they hurry on to the related concerns of literary study before adequately mastering the techniques of analysis and criticism of texts. And probably every teacher, at some time or other, has found himself "talking around" the text rather than discussing the text itself. "Start with the text" is a maxim that no student of literature should forget.

Granted, then, that one starts with the text, what is it he gets from the text? What does he look for? For one thing, he looks for ideas, attitudes, feelings, which often are presented directly, as in essays, but which more frequently are presented indirectly, that is, are embodied in poems, stories, or plays. A great deal of human experience is recorded in literature, and certainly one value we derive from studying literature is an increased acquaintance with man's intellectual, emotional, and spiritual experience.

No one would deny that value in literature, but it is not the only value. Indeed, if we extract the ideas from an imaginative work, we often find them not very remarkable. Elizabethan sonnets, for example, say over and over again, "I love you," "You are very beautiful," "My verse will immortalize you," and so on; no one would argue that they are great poems because of the ideas or feelings they present. A line of Alexander Pope, if we extract the so-called basic meaning, may say simply that so-and-so is a rascal or a dunce. Calling people names is something anyone can do. Pope's reputation as a satirist rests on something more than the fact that he called people names. Or again, Browning's poem "Andrea del Sarto" contains the lines "Ah, but a man's reach should exceed his grasp, Or what's a heaven for?"—which could be paraphrased to read: Perfection in any endeavor is impossible in this life, but that fact should not keep one from striving for perfection. It is an interesting idea, which one can contemplate and perhaps choose to incorporate in his own conduct. But the poem is more than this idea, together with other ideas that can be extracted from it. A discussion of the poem that was limited to the ideas in it would be something like a criticism of a Renaissance painting of the Crucifixion that discussed only the religious significance of Christ's death. In short, what a literary work says is more than the so-called essential ideas and feelings it states or embodies. Or, we can say that *what* a work says is only a part of its message. Equally important—perhaps, for students of literature, more important, since it is peculiarly a literary matter—is *how* the work says it.

To distinguish sharply among these five approaches to literary study may seem to be a pedantic or semiphilosophic analysis that bears little relation to our actual practice. It is true, of course, that in the process of our own reading, in classroom experience, and in written literary commentary we find that the approaches are often mixed. This is as it should be, since the approaches are closely related and can profitably be used in conjunction with each other. A critic, for instance, often needs to know literary history. In analyzing a poem he may err from not knowing how a certain word was used in an earlier day, or even from not knowing so humble a fact as a date. Again, it has been shown that *Tom Sawyer* is in part a burlesque of moralistic juvenile literature, and that the structure of the book is designed to achieve this end. Professor Walter Blair, who made this critical observation, was able to make it because he had studied the writings that Mark Twain was familiar with and was burlesquing. A knowledge of literary history, in other words, suggested the critical insight. But however interdependent the approaches to literature are, it is helpful to distinguish them in our minds. In our study we may wish, especially as we gain literary experience, to combine approaches, but it is most desirable to know with some exactness what it is we are combining.

Although, as we have seen, each approach to literature has its own value, probably the textual approach (section 5, above) should claim most of the attention of the elementary student. He can study backgrounds without much help, and he needs little instruction to enable him to "work up" the facts of biography and literary history. Textual analysis and criticism, however, are another matter. It is here that classroom instruction —and, it is hoped, the present pamphlet—can be of help.

It is sometimes argued that elementary literary study should not be concerned with technique, on the grounds that the study of technique is difficult and dull, and is therefore better deferred to a later time. Literary analysis, it is true, is not a simple procedure, but the elements involved in it are surely not beyond the capacity of students who can handle the intricacies of chemistry, economics, or philosophy. Nor is technique a dull matter if one can be shown that it enhances his understanding of what he reads. As for deferring its study until a later time, the trouble is that advanced courses do not teach elements, but rather assume a certain familiarity with them.

One hears the argument, too, that technique need not concern the "general student," who wants some acquaintance with literature, but who does not intend to pursue his literary study beyond an elementary course. This belief rests on the assumption that technique is something superimposed on a body of material; one can study and appreciate the material, it is held, without worrying about the superimposed technique. But technique is not "superimposed" on subject matter in the best writing. The *way* a thing is said is a part of *what* is said. In a real sense, then, to ignore technique is to miss part of the substance of a literary work. The justification for studying literature in a college class is that such study can help us to read more perceptively, and hence increase our understanding and enjoyment of what we read. One way, probably the most important way, in which it can help is to acquaint us with the rudiments of literary technique.

THE ROLE OF CRITICISM

The discussion so far has been concerned with ways of studying literature. Although such study involves a lot of hard thinking, it is, in a sense, a receptive process. We study in order to understand. But there comes a time in a college course when one is expected to demonstrate his understanding by saying something about the literature he has been studying. When one makes such a statement he is engaging in criticism, however humble his efforts may be. Criticism is not mere faultfinding. Rather, it is a discussion that seeks to describe, analyze, or evaluate a literary work. Its function is to illuminate the work for the benefit of other readers. The function is a useful one, for no reader is so accomplished that he cannot profit from perceptive comments by a skilled critic. There have been few truly great critics in the past, and a student may feel it unfair to be asked to enter such a difficult field. But it is not really an impossible requirement, for no teacher expects profound criticism from a beginning student; all that is asked is that he make an honest and conscientious effort. Since one only half knows a thing unless he can tell what he knows, he should read not passively but in the expectation that he will make statements about what he reads. What kind of statements? This, of course, is the crucial question, which cannot be answered simply. The rest of this chapter treats some general critical matters, but more detailed suggestions appear in the several following chapters, since elementary criticism is a major subject of this entire book.

The kinds of critical statements we can make are those growing out of the kinds of study outlined above. If one were criticizing *Huckleberry*

Finn, he could build a discussion around the way the book affected him —showing what parts amused him, terrified him, saddened him, angered him, and so on. If done well, such a statement might manage to say several interesting things about the book. We would call it impressionistic criticism. Or, one could discuss how the book revealed the author. By citing and interpreting properly the episodes that exhibit human follies and depravities, as well as virtues, one could write an interesting critique of the book that would consist of an essay on Mark Twain's view of human nature. Again, one might wish to discuss the way the book reveals the social life of mid-America before the Civil War. He could speak of the various social classes represented, from Huck's Pap to the aristocratic Grangerfords, the several social types seen on and along the River and their customs, habits, and attitudes; and he would want to say something about the dominating social fact of slavery.

Such discussions of *Huckleberry Finn* would be criticism in the broad sense. Criticism in the more restricted sense would focus not on reader, writer, or social background, but rather on the book itself. It might begin by describing the general nature of the story—a boy escaped from a tyrannical father teams up with a runaway slave, and as the two float downstream on a raft they encounter many experiences. It would probably continue by analyzing the story, that is, by noting its component parts. These might be segments of the narrative—individual chapters, or groups of chapters. Or they might be such technical elements as theme, setting, language, and point of view (the fact that Huck is the narrator throughout). All, or the most significant, of these parts could be discussed individually and their relationship to one another shown. When the parts of a work fit together harmoniously, or when means are well adapted to ends, we are inclined to say the work is a successful artistic whole. So, for instance, in the episode where Huck struggles with his conscience over whether to turn Jim in, the implicit satire against the institution of slavery is greatly enhanced by the technical feature of point of view, and it is that which makes for irony—Huck, as narrator, failing to see the implications of his actions. On the other hand, many readers find the last portion of the book relatively weak, chiefly because the tone and atmosphere as well as the characters of the principals are not consistent with those elements in the earlier part of the story.

Personal preferences may creep into criticism of this sort, but the critic who views the work for itself seeks to be objective in his observations. In broad terms we can say that he is concerned with two things, not singly but in their relationship. These two things are known as content and form, or matter and manner, or substance and technique—or, we might say simply, the what and the how. What a writer says is of course important; but equally important is *how* he says it. Sometimes we feel that what a writer says is so valuable that we are willing to overlook his carelessness in saying it; conversely, some writers of thin substance have been admired for the richness or grace of their expression. The best literary works—and this is one reason why they are the best—are those whose form not only is well adapted to their content but also helps to shape it. Too often readers are content with seeking the pure substance of a work. We need also to recognize *how* the substance, or content, is handled, and, where possible, to determine wherein and to what extent the handling, or form, is appropriate to the substance. To cite an example, we can speak of the content of *Othello* as being a series of actions revealing marital jealousy; and we can make statements about the form or structure of the play—the expository first act (a little drama in itself) serving as a kind of prologue, and the absence of a subplot in the following acts serving both to speed up the tempo of the action and also to rule out distractions from the central action. Such observations about structure are fairly significant by themselves, but they are much more so if one goes on to say that these structural features are particularly appropriate to the substance of the play. The drive toward the catastrophe in this play of jealousy must be steady and swift. In short, the form is admirably suited to the content.

Literary criticism of this kind is often quite detailed and complex; the critic may see many significances in a work and may point to various features, qualities, and relationships that are not at all apparent to the casual reader. When one encounters such criticism, in print or in the classroom, he may feel that it is a revealing commentary on the work in question. On the other hand, he may be skeptical; if asked his opinion, he may say, "This comment is all very well, but I'm not sure the critic isn't reading things into the work. Is he sure the author intended to express all these meanings?" Two separate matters are involved here.

As to the first, whether the critic is "reading things into" the work, there can be no general answer; sometimes he is and sometimes he is not. The test must be, Is his comment really supported by the text? Criticism cannot be irresponsible. The critic must prove his case before the bar of intelligent, experienced readers. Of course the critic *may* be reading things into the text. If his discussion is incomplete, or is unsupported by the text—in short, if he does not prove his case—then we do right to be skeptical. But simply because a critic makes an observation that has not occurred to us before, we must not necessarily conclude that his comments are invalid. Readers vary greatly in intellect, literary experience, and insight. What is obvious to one reader may seem intricate or farfetched to another. Indeed, the function of criticism is to show us things we had not seen before.

The second point involved in the remark of the skeptical reader has to do with the author's intention. Did the author, when he wrote, have in mind all the things the critic says are in the work? Did he really intend them to be there? The fact is that with most literary works we simply do not know what the author intended, other than what he says in the work. Writers theorize about their art, but they usually make little comment about their intention in particular works. They feel, quite properly, that the work makes its own statement, and that if they had wanted to say the thing differently they would have done so. When we do have the author's comment on a work, in notebooks, letters, prefaces, and so forth, we should make use of it. Often it sheds light on his method of creation or provides hints for interpreting the work.

Ultimately, however, we must be concerned not with what the author was trying to do but with what he did. It is conceivable that he achieved something different from what he intended; both Melville and Thomas Wolfe insisted on this point. The extreme and familiar instance is the student talking over a test paper with his teacher; "What I meant was . . . ," he will say, and the teacher will reply, "Yes, but what you wrote is something different." Criticism and creation, though related, are different processes. The critic is concerned with what is on the page, however it may have got there. It is for this reason that it is probably a mistake, as we set out to comment critically on a work, to begin with what we regard as the author's purpose, proceeding to show how the parts of the work help to achieve that purpose. Instead of following this procedure, which is based on what has been called the "intentional fallacy," we will do better to speak only of the work as it stands, and to assume nothing at all about the writer's intention.

The discussion in this chapter has tried to orient readers to the task of systematic literary study and of criticism based on that study. The following chapters treat these matters in some detail. Let us remember, as we proceed, that the ideal reader is an attentive reader. He reads closely and infers meanings. How much a careful reader can infer is suggested in Sean O'Faolain's comment on a short story:

> Take the following example. It is the opening of Chekov's story *The Lady with the Dog*. Here is the first sentence:—"It was reported that a new face had been seen on the quay; a lady with a little dog."
>
> The amount of information conveyed in that sentence is an interesting example of the shorthand of the modern short story. What do we gather from it: "It was reported that a new face had been seen on the quay; a lady with a little dog." We gather, altogether by implication, that the scene is laid in a port. We gather that this port is a seaside resort, for ladies with little dogs do not perambulate on commercial docks. We gather that the season is fine weather —probably summer or autumn. We gather that this seaside resort is a sleepy, unfrequented little place: for one does not observe new faces at big, crowded places like Brighton or Deauville. Furthermore, the phrase "it was reported" implies that gossip circulates in a friendly way at this sleepy resort. We gather still more. We gather that somebody has been bored and wakes up at this bit of gossip; and that we shall presently hear about him. I say "him," because one again guesses, when it is a question of a lady, that the person most likely

to be interested is a man. And sure enough the next sentence confirms all this. "Dimitri Gomov who had been a fortnight at Yalta and got used to it . . ." And so on.

We may imagine how much time it would take, and how boring it would be to have all that told at length. This compression by suggestion and implication is one of the great charms of the modern short story. . . .[1]

One does not easily become as perceptive a reader as Mr. O'Faolain, but his inferences show what it is possible to derive from a single sentence. He gives us a mark to shoot at.

The ideal reader also approaches literature in the proper attitude. There are extremes in this matter. One student, because of his inexperience, will defer completely to the opinions of those he considers authorities—authors of books and articles, his teacher, and so on. A second student will insist that since literature is a subjective matter, one person's opinion is as good as another's. Neither attitude is altogether the proper one, although the second is perhaps the healthier because it usually reflects a lively interest. We need a certain frankness and boldness in discussing literature, but we must avoid critical irresponsibility. Perhaps we can say that the ideal attitude is one of honesty and courage, tempered with humility.

For Further Reading

Daiches, David. *A Study of Literature*. Ithaca, N. Y.: Cornell University Press, 1948.
Wellek, René, and Austin Warren. *Theory of Literature*. 2nd ed. New York: Harcourt, Brace, 1955. (Harvest Books)

[1] Sean O'Faolain, *The Short Story* (New York: Devin-Adair, 1951), pp. 151-152. Quoted by permission of the publisher.

• II •
FICTION

THE NATURE OF FICTION

Human beings are insatiably curious about themselves. We are forever interested to learn what people are doing—in our families, our towns, our country, our world—and what they have done in the past. We learn about people by observing them, but we are also eager to hear reports of other people's observations. "Tell me a story" is the plea not only of children but of men and women in all countries and in all ages. Storytellers in both prose and verse have answered the plea in fables, folk tales, ballads, epics, romances, down to the complex forms of novel and short story in more recent times. The present chapter discusses the features common to these forms of fiction.

Long ago, storytellers recounted the exploits of heroes, drawing on known facts about these flesh and blood people, but also embroidering on the facts. Their stories were thus a blend of fact and fancy. In later times we have come to distinguish between these two kinds of narrative, calling one history and the other fiction. Aristotle marked the difference between the two in a distinction that we still observe: history, he said, "describes the thing that has been," whereas fiction describes "a kind of thing that might be." History deals in particulars, unique persons and events, that will never be repeated exactly. Fiction, says Aristotle, deals with "universals"; it makes statements about what a certain kind of man or woman "will probably or necessarily say or do." In dealing with universals, fiction resembles philosophy; but in presenting the universal through the particular (specific characters and events), it resembles history. The realm of fiction, then, lies between the realm of history and the realm of philosophy.

We know that the particulars of fiction, unlike those of history, are "made up," or imagined; the word "fiction" means something invented, fashioned, imagined. It is perhaps natural, therefore, that we think of history as true, and fiction as mere fabrication, or, at bottom, false. But these terms "true" and "false" are misleading. True and false to what?

In saying that history is true and fiction false we say only that history treats what actually happened in the past, insofar as it can be determined, whereas fiction does not. But in another sense fiction can be quite true: it can be, as we say, true to human nature, or, as Hawthorne said, it can show the "truth of the human heart."

Consider the history of a person, that is, a biography. The biographer tells us what a man did, and he tries to determine why he did these things— that is, he tries to suggest motives, or causes, for his actions. But because he must stick to facts, his statements of causation will probably be tentative and incomplete, and will be limited to one man. A novelist, on the other hand, can give a full, meaningful account of a character's motives, an account which, because the character is representative and universal, tells us a good deal about human beings *in general*. Or again, contrast fiction not with history but with life. We may think we know another person well, but actually there is a great deal we can never know about even close friends. Not only are they unwilling to reveal all—they do not know all, and could not express it if they did. But a good novelist can explain everything, or at least all that is necessary in a given situation. For this reason we can say that we know more *of significance* about Catherine Earnshaw in Emily Brontë's *Wuthering Heights,* Eustacia Vye in Thomas Hardy's *The Return of the Native,* Tom Joad in John Steinbeck's *The Grapes of Wrath,* or Huckleberry Finn than we know about most of our acquaintances. Reading fiction is vicarious experience, but it is experience that often goes further and deeper than that of actual life, either as lived or as reported in history. In this sense fiction is most certainly "true."

Another way of considering the truth of fiction is in terms of the *kind* of truth it reveals. Some novelists and story writers, particularly in the last hundred years, have recorded with great accuracy the outward features of life. They show us the clothes, room furnishings, and other objects surrounding characters, and they take pains to make their characters' speech authentic, that is, like the speech of actual people. Stories that render faithfully these outward circumstances of life we call *realistic* because they are true to reality, or, to put it more accurately, to actuality. "Actuality" is the better term to describe the appearances of the world, for we often feel that reality is found elsewhere than in appearances— found, for instance, in psychological and moral truths. On the other hand, writers primarily concerned with these inner truths often do little to picture life as it is in its external forms. These two kinds of fiction (we are speaking of extremes; there are, of course, shadings and overlappings) once were called, respectively, novel and romance, or, as we say today, the realistic novel and the romantic novel. Hawthorne pointed the distinction: the novel, he said, aimed "at a very minute fidelity, not merely to the possible, but to the probable and ordinary course of man's experience"; the romance, concerned with truth of the human heart, "presents that truth under circumstances . . . of the writer's own choosing or creation." Of course, both kinds of novel have value and both present truths, though of different kinds. We are so accustomed today to the realistic mode, however, that if we are to read a romantic novel profitably and fairly, we must be reminded to read and judge it on its own terms.

The usual way of analyzing fiction is to consider its components—plot, character, setting, and so on. In a way this is a process of fragmentation, quite different from the wholeness of impression we receive when we read. This fragmentation bothered the novelist and critic Henry James, who felt it tended to suggest that the elements existed in the story in isolation: here we have character, here we have plot, and so on. Actually, James says, all the elements are related: "What is character but the determination of incident? What is incident but the illustration of character?" He is, of course, quite right, as he so often is in his brilliant essay "The Art of Fiction." But we still can safely discuss a story in terms of the traditional elements, if we make a special effort to see them as related to one another. As a matter of fact, it is hard not to see them as related. If, for instance, we begin to say what kind of man Sinclair Lewis's Babbitt is (character), we soon are talking about what he does (plot) in the city of Zenith (setting), and what his actions and speech (dialogue) enable the author to say by way of satirical commentary (theme). Analysis of the story into its elements simply allows us to talk about one thing at a time.

A discussion of these fictional elements follows. Much of it applies to all kinds of fiction. But because the short story poses problems of its own, it is treated further in a following section. Additional hints on reading fiction are given in Chapter V.

THE ELEMENTS OF FICTION

Character

It is remarkable how a writer, by putting words on paper, can create characters that seem real to us. When the job is well done we feel that the characters are vivid and believable, that they "come to life." Even a moderately close reading of a story enables us to feel the vital force of a character. To be able to discuss the character, however, we need to see how the writer presents him and to understand our corresponding obligations as readers.

REVELATION OF CHARACTER

A writer reveals character in several different ways. One usual classification groups them as *direct* and *indirect:* when the trait itself is mentioned, by the author or by another character (for example, "He is a mean old skinflint"), we have direct characterization; when only the behavior (speech, actions, and so on) from which we infer traits is given, we have indirect characterization, the method preferred by more recent writers.

A somewhat different classification may be clearer: those methods that resemble the ways in which character is revealed to us *in life,* and those that are possible only *in literature.* In the following list, methods 1–4 fall in the former group, methods 5–6 in the latter.

1. *Characterization by the Reactions of Other Characters.* Just as in life our opinion of a person is often influenced by what others say about him and how they act toward him, so in fiction. One character may call another "an old skinflint"; or, merely by his actions and attitudes he can tell us about him. In *Moby-Dick* young Ishmael, who wants to go whaling but as yet knows nothing about Captain Ahab of the *Pequod,* talks with one of the ship's owners:

> "Want to see what whaling is, eh? Have ye clapped eye on Captain Ahab?"
> "Who is Captain Ahab, sir?"
> "Aye, aye, I thought so. Captain Ahab is the Captain of this ship."

The owner's remark "I thought so" implies a good deal; spelled out it means "I felt sure, when you said you wanted to go whaling, that you didn't know Captain Ahab; if you knew him you probably wouldn't be so eager to sign on his ship." Although the remark does not characterize Ahab definitely and directly, it suggests how the owner feels about him— suggests that Ahab has a reputation and is a man to be reckoned with. Characterization of this kind is common in fiction. Of course, when we encounter it in a story we must weigh the reliability of the person doing the characterizing, for fiction here is like life: the credibility of testimony— in court or in our everyday affairs—depends upon the trustworthiness of the person giving it. The testimony of characters who are naïve, ignorant, or biased is valuable, but we have to discount or qualify much that they say.

2. *Characterization by Externals.* Again in fiction as in life we judge people not only by what we hear but by what we see: (a) A character's *physical appearance* can reveal things about his nature. It is true, as psychologists tell us, that appearances are often deceptive. Persons confronted with mixed photographs of rogues and solid citizens will not always make the proper identifications; and we have met shifty-eyed people who were not untrustworthy, as well as people who look us squarely in the eye and lie outrageously. Nevertheless we do associate character with appearance, and so does fiction. Writers tell us a good deal when they indicate a character's facial features, build or figure, posture, gait, and so on. (b) A character's *surroundings* (clothes, possessions) are also revealing. A description mentioning Johnny Doe's turned-up collar, low-slung Levi's, and the sonorous muffler on his car might be lost on the general reader, but teen-agers would know how to place Johnny. Or think how much we learn of a character's taste, education, and background by being told he is reading *True Confessions*—or *The Atlantic Monthly,* or *The Partisan Review*

Such details will not individualize a character, but they put him in a group, and hence set him off from many other people.

3. *Characterization by Speech.* It is plain that a person, or a fictional character, reveals himself in his speech: "Everybody thought him smart," the saying goes, "until he opened his mouth." Many modern realistic writers have learned to capture human speech with incredible accuracy. Besides giving an air of actuality to a story, well-rendered speech tells a great deal about a character. Through his speech we learn his thoughts, opinions, attitudes, and feelings. Equally important with what he says is how he says it. His grammar, sentence structure, vocabulary—in fact, all the elements of style—not only show his social and educational level but also, and more importantly, show how his mind works. A similar revelation is afforded by a character's written style. The eighteenth-century epistolary novels (stories told entirely through personal letters) make use of the device, as does John P. Marquand's *The Late George Apley.*

4. *Characterization by Action.* This indirect method of characterization, together with number 3, probably does more than any other method to reveal character. Clearly, what a character does—or fails to do or chooses *not* to do—reflects his character, just as in life we say that actions speak louder than words. Perhaps the only difficulty here is that we may become so engrossed in the action of the story that we forget to make the full inference about character. In analyzing an action we should ask, "What kind of person is it that would do a thing like that?" or, simply, "What traits of character does the action reveal?"

5. *Characterization by the Author's Statement.* In life we learn about people by keeping our eyes and ears open, but there is nobody standing by to interpret people's actions and character for us. Fiction, however, is not life but a representation of it, presented by an author, one of whose privileges is to explain what is going on in the world he creates. Earlier writers in particular availed themselves of the privilege; Fielding and Thackeray, for instance, speak freely to the reader about their characters. This direct method is the method of the essay, as when Addison discusses Sir Roger de Coverley. The indirect method resembles that of the drama, where all is done through speech and action, and the playwright can never address us directly. Most novelists use both methods, although modern fiction has come to rely more and more heavily on the indirect method. Henry James objected to the direct, essaylike way of presenting character on the ground that it tends to destroy the illusion that fiction seeks to create: we see the puppet master manipulating the strings of his dolls. Many writers and readers today share James's opinion. Granted it can be argued that although fiction seeks and is often able to create the illusion of reality, we know it *is* an illusion, just as we know a dramatic performance creates an illusion and consequently do not personally attack the villain. Perhaps the real reason we value indirect characterization is that

we enjoy the participation involved in making inferences from behavior. We enjoy the older writers, too, however, even when they "intrude" on the story. They often have interesting things to say, and we enjoy weighing our judgments against theirs.

6. *Characterization by Revelation of a Character's Thoughts.* Here, too, the novelist can reveal more than life does: he can tell us what his people are thinking. Sometimes this is put in the form of an indirect statement ("With all now gone, Georgiana wondered what would become of her"), sometimes in the form of direct statement (" 'I haven't a thing,' Georgiana thought; 'What ever will I do? Where can I turn?' "). Either kind of statement can be greatly expanded. In fact, older fiction made much use of this kind of mental analysis, often devoting lengthy passages and even whole chapters to it. The analogy with other literary types applies here, too; the indirect statement is like the essay, the direct statement is like a soliloquy in a play. An extended passage of introspection cast in direct statement is sometimes called an *interior monologue*. The passage reveals the character's thoughts, but they are presented, though usually without quotation marks, as though he were speaking them to himself.

Because such introspective analyses, whether presented directly or indirectly, purport to represent the workings of a character's mind, the details in them are often loosely arranged. In retrospection one's mind does not work systematically, but rather mulls things over, with one thought leading to another and perhaps returning on itself. A writer may try to show this mental process by discarding normal expression in favor of an expression that suggests the way the mind works. Instead of a succession of well-rounded sentences, he may use parts of sentences (fragments and isolated phrases) which ignore the rules of syntax, and he may emphasize this odd sentence structure with various devices of punctuation (dashes, italics, periods to indicate omissions, parentheses, and so on).

Such unconventional expression is often used to represent what is called the *stream of consciousness*. But applied to fiction, the phrase "stream of consciousness" refers not so much to how a character's thinking is rendered on the page as to what is involved in his thinking. The writers who have rendered the stream of consciousness most successfully—James Joyce, Virginia Woolf, William Faulkner—all start from an assumption about the human mind that is grounded in the findings of modern psychologists, particularly those of Sigmund Freud. What we ordinarily consider as the mind, Freud held, is only a part of it, the *conscious* mind; there is also the *unconscious,* a portion of mind that is active and influential on conduct, but the workings of which are largely unknown to the conscious mind. As we speak of the two parts of an iceberg, the visible part and the much larger part beneath the surface, so with the mind. It is this part of the mind "beneath the surface" that stream of consciousness writers explore. And because the unconscious mind does not operate with words and sentences but with images and symbols, so the writer uses these nonverbal terms of "thought," which he must present to us through words. Stream of consciousness writing is a complicated matter. As has been suggested, it is much more than the illogical jumble it appears to be. It represents an effort of novelists to carry a step further one of the universal concerns of fiction, the exploration of the individual human being.

It would be a mistake to think that a novelist or a story writer confines himself to one of these methods of revealing character; ordinarily he uses them in combination. It would be wrong, too, to think that one method is absolutely or necessarily better than another, for each is good in its own way. One final word should be said: The entire matter of character revelation is closely related to the technical matter of *point of view*. A writer's choice of ways of characterizing his people is often strictly determined by the point of view he assumes as a storyteller. It would be helpful, therefore, to review the preceding section carefully after studying the section later in this chapter on point of view.

UNDERSTANDING CHARACTER

The chief question we ask in studying character in fiction is, What kind of person is the author presenting? As suggested above, the author provides us with several kinds of data, from which we infer character. Making the inference is a process of abstraction; from the concrete action, speech, or description we infer the abstract trait embodied in the actor. If a dowager says, "No, no, it would be quite impossible to see them socially. He's in *trade;* he keeps a sort of shop, I believe," we infer she is *proud, haughty,* and *class-conscious.* One senses these traits as he reads, even though he may not give names to them. But we must give names to them if we are to discuss the character. Finding appropriate terms to denote character traits is therefore an important part of our study.

Another important question to ask about a character is, What function does he perform in the story? Why, that is, is he in the story at all? What exactly does he contribute to it? Since the function of the major characters is plain, their concerns forming the substance of the story, this question of function applies more particularly to minor characters, who can contribute to a story in several ways. Sometimes they simply round out the picture, that is, people the world the novelist creates. Sometimes they perform necessary actions in the plot, such as helping or hindering the central character in his pursuits. Sometimes they are involved in only subordinate action, which nevertheless may be useful in shedding light on some facet of the main character's personality. Often such a character serves as *confidant* (the feminine form is *confidante*), one who is sympathetic with a main character, and who may draw him out in conversation— a lifelike way of revealing his thoughts. Or he may serve more as a *foil,* a contrasting character, whose behavior, attitudes, and opinions, different from those of the main character, serve to define and emphasize the latter by means of contrast. To sum up, it is important to determine a character's *function* as well as his nature.

Plot

Keeping in mind that fictional elements are closely related (a man is what he does, and does what he is), let us consider what we mean by plot. Sometimes the word is used loosely to mean simply what happens in a story. "Tell me the plot," we say, and what we may get is a detailed particularized recital of events in the story—really a *résumé* of the action, or a *summary*. Or if our informer is experienced, he may give us a succinct, generalized account (an *epitome*) that presents the gist of the story. This is closer to plot in the stricter sense of the word, especially if the gist is seen to involve a conflict, for by plot in literary discussion we usually mean a *pattern of actions involving conflict*.

PLOT AS CONFLICT

Although it is sometimes said that there is a potential story in every set of happenings, this is hardly true. Merely stringing together all the events of a day in one's life, for instance, would not necessarily make a story. We feel that to make a story these events would have to have point, a focus, the most common form of which is some sort of conflict.

1. *Kinds of Conflict.* We think of conflict as physical opposition in the form of duels, gun fights, slam-bang free-for-alls, but of course the sword, gun, or fist is only an instrument. It is an instrument of the will, and an individual human will can encounter conflicts of various kinds— one individual against another, an individual against a group (his family, town, society, and so on), an individual against nature or against his social and economic environment. As soon as we detect the nature of the conflict in a story, we align the characters on either side of the issue. We see that they are not isolated but are related meaningfully to one another in terms of the conflict; or, in the jargon of the young, we have the "good guys" and the "bad guys." In serious fiction, it hardly need be said, the alignment, as well as the moral differentiation, is not so simple. Sometimes, indeed, part of the interest of a story lies in discovering allegiances that at first are not clear, or in observing shifts of allegiance. We should recognize, too, that although we have been speaking of *the* conflict, often there are several. Separate groups may be involved in conflicts, or one man may be involved in several conflicts: he may, for instance, be in conflict with another man, with all or part of his family, and with himself. Working out such relationships is an important first step in the study of plot.

2. *The Course of the Conflict.* When one first encounters Aristotle's

statement that a story has "a beginning, a middle, and an end," he may feel it to be obvious, yet it states the essential portions of a plot. The opening part of a story, called the *exposition,* acquaints us with the characters and shows us their condition in a certain setting. The characters may be doing things, but for a while we do not know what their actions are leading to. Before long, however, a situation develops that promises conflict. This situation and those that follow it develop the conflict in the section of the story called the *complication,* usually the longest portion of the story. The *climax* occurs when it becomes clear which way the conflict will be resolved, and the final part of the story—the *denouement,* or *resolution*—shows how the conflict is settled.

It is easy to recognize these main parts of the action in a typical Western, which is to say that it has a clear, simple, and obvious plot. Most serious fiction is more complicated. Furthermore, merely discovering the main parts of a story and calling them by name tells us little about the story; rather it is a starting point for discussion. In considering the exposition, for instance, we note what possibilities for action lie in the initial situation; and of episodes in the complication we ask, among other things, how each of them contributes to the development of the conflict—where, that is, as a result of the episode, the character stands with respect to the conflict.

Sometimes it helps us grasp the structure of the story if we think of the plot development in terms of a diagram. There are no set rules to follow here. In general we can plot (in a different but related sense of the word) the action in terms of the fortunes of the central character, that is, where he stands in relation to the conflict in which he is engaged. So, for a story showing the progressive degradation and defeat of a character we would have a descending curve; for a success story, an ascending curve; for a story showing a character triumphing only after severe difficulties, we would have a low curve that rises sharply at the end; for a story showing a character succeeding up to a point and then failing, we would have a *reversal,* and the curve would be mostly high but would drop sharply at the end. Drawing such curves will not tell us a great deal, and it would be easy to make them overelaborate. But they do help us to grasp the course of a story's plot by visualizing it.

When a character experiences actions that seriously affect his fortunes (including his thoughts, feelings, attitudes), he may learn from the experience and so be a somewhat different person at the end of the story from what he is at the beginning. Such change, in fact, is often an important feature of a story. A character who changes significantly in this way is called a *developing* character, as distinguished from a *static* character, who remains the same kind of person throughout the story. We require that a change in character be convincing, and this leads us to several other features of plot that we can include under the term *probability*.

PROBABILITY OF ACTIONS

There are several words that we all use in speaking of an action in a story: we say it is *convincing, believable, credible, likely, plausible,* or *probable.* All of these terms refer to an action's fidelity, not to what has been, but to what *might be.* We use them often (and, for inferior fiction, their opposites) because we feel that truth in fiction is of crucial importance—the truth of human nature, as we spoke of it earlier. As readers perhaps we all have something of the skeptic in us. Knowing that fiction is not life but a representation of it, we are not willing to accept automatically whatever the writer tells us. It is true that if we read with the proper sympathy we stand ready to be convinced, but we require that the author make his story plausible or probable. If he presents strange or unusual things, the reader may feel that the author is exceeding his rights as a fabricator and is telling what is unlikely. One might be more inclined to react in this way toward realistic writing than toward romance, for in reading romance we are willing to grant the author what Hawthorne called more "latitude" in introducing the "marvelous."

But all of this does not mean that a writer is required to stick to the usual and ordinary. He is at liberty, of course, to introduce unusual characters and actions, but—and this is the point—he must take pains to make them seem probable. They will not seem probable merely because they are drawn from life, for many remarkable things happen in life which in fiction would seem quite improbable (for example, Bobby Thomson's game- and pennant-winning, ninth inning, 2-out, bases-loaded home run for the Giants in 1951). "Truth," as the saying has it, "is stranger than fiction." A writer makes his characters and actions seem probable by the way he tells his story—in short, by technique, some features of which we can consider.

1. *Handling of Time.* We have all seen a half-hour television show in which a character who for 25 minutes has been a complete no-good says, in effect, in the last few minutes, "I see I have been wrong in trying to murder my aunt; from now on I plan to lead a blameless life." We moan, not because reformations in life are improbable, but because this one is unprepared for (a point to be considered in a moment) and because it happens so suddenly. In life such a change in character usually takes time, and fiction, to create the illusion of life, must suggest the passage of time. This is not simply a matter of referring to the calendar, for it is not actual calendar time that is important, but the *effect* of time. This may be achieved by a shift in point of view, as in the old epistolary novels. It may be achieved by inserting episodes involving characters other than the central ones, so that when we return to the central characters we *feel* that sufficient time has passed to allow for change in character. Our sense of time is affected also by the method used to tell the story—straight narra-

tive, scene, analysis, and description. The rough formula for a given passage is this: the sense of time's passing is proportionate to the progress of the story in relation to the space devoted to the passage (that is, the number of lines or pages, and hence the reading time). So, straight narrative can advance the action rapidly in relatively few words; scene, or dramatized narrative with dialogue, can advance it slowly (though vividly); and analysis and description may not advance it at all—which is why some readers skip what they consider tedious passages of description: they hold up the progress of the story. In such ways a novelist can manipulate fictional time to increase the probability of character changes and of actions.

2. *Motivation.* By motivation we mean the reasons a character acts the way he does. We want to know what he does, but we also want to know why he does it. Motives can be plainly stated or they can be subtly implied, but if they are absent altogether we are likely to feel that the work is somehow not true and convincing—that it lacks probability.

Motives are suggested to us in several ways. The author may mention them briefly or, as many nineteenth-century novelists did (George Eliot, Thomas Hardy, Henry James), he may discuss them at length in passages of analysis. The character in question may state his own motives or another character may state them, though in both cases we must be on the lookout for false motives; a character may, as we all do in life, *rationalize* his behavior. That is, he may give good reasons for his actions, but reasons that at bottom are not the real ones, which may, as we have seen, be located in his unconscious mind. The chief way in which motive is suggested, however, is through character. If we know the character well enough—know his desires, his scale of values, and the way his mind works—we feel, when he performs an action, that the explanation of his conduct lies in the kind of person he is. He is the kind of person who *would do* what he does.

This matter of probability sometimes presents a problem. We have all heard people say, "I don't believe a man would act the way this character acts." Is it a fair objection? To answer the question one must ask what it assumes. When the speaker says "a man" he implies an actual, flesh and blood person; it is therefore apparent that he is assuming that the character should act like an actual person, and is objecting to the action of the character because he does not so act. In a word, he is testing the action by life.

Now we value "lifelike" portrayal in fiction so highly that this test seems perfectly natural and legitimate, and in a way it is. But it presents difficulties. Our personal experience, particularly if we are young, is limited; in fact, one reason we read fiction is to extend our experience. Often we simply do not know enough about what people do, and why, to be able to say, with assurance, that such and such an action is not lifelike. Then too, what would we say, for example, about the story of Oedipus in Sophocles' Greek tragedy? Oedipus put out his eyes when he discovered he had married his mother. We cannot test *this* action by experience.

Take another example from the drama, Shakespeare's *Othello*. Desdemona, a Venetian girl, elopes against her father's wishes with a dark-skinned Moor, who later, suspecting her of infidelity, kills her. Suppose a reader objects to the elopement, saying, "I don't believe a white girl would have married a Moor." We meet the objection, not by arguing that such things do happen in life (although they do), but by showing that Shakespeare took pains to give reasons, or motives, for Desdemona's choice of a mate; briefly, she was charmed by Othello's moving account of his exciting past. We justify the action of her elopement, then, not by testing it according to life, but by noting that the author made the action plausible by presenting a clear motive.

Probability of this kind we call *inherent probability,* since it derives from elements in the work itself. Often this kind of probability coincides with probability to life; we justify an action in fiction both because it is like life as we know it, and also because it seems consistent with what the author tells us about the character. A case in point would be the actions of Tom Sawyer. But the two kinds of probability will perhaps not coincide in stories remote from our personal experience. In reading such stories, indeed in reading all stories, we should look for the justification of an action *within the work itself.*

3. *Foreshadowing.* The term "foreshadowing" refers to information presented in an early part of a story that tends to make us accept as probable an event occurring in a later part. Character itself might in a sense be regarded as a kind of foreshadowing, but the term is usually used for specific statements or events. In *Moby-Dick,* for instance, statements by various mariners about the terrific destructive power of the White Whale, or revelations of their fearful attitude toward him, serve to foreshadow the outcome of Ahab's duel with the Whale; that is, they prepare for the later action by telling us what we can probably expect from Moby Dick. Melville was obliged to introduce a good deal of foreshadowing, he says, so that we would not regard the final destruction of the *Pequod* as something prodigious or fantastic, but would accept it as something imaginatively quite true. Foreshadowing, then, increases the probability of the final action.

It is sometimes said that foreshadowing should not be too plentiful or too obvious, lest it rob us of the pleasure of surprise when the foreshadowed event occurs. This is a sound principle, but it applies especially to stories in which the turn of events is, of itself, of great interest. In mystery stories too much foreshadowing destroys the *suspense*. But "suspense" can be taken to mean more than that feature of a story which creates in us an excited curiosity about the outcome. We can feel suspense in a story even when, for any of several reasons, including generous foreshadowing, we are sure of the outcome. So it must have been with the Greeks, watching their tragedies. These plays were based on familiar stories of famous families, and the chorus, oracles, and other devices provided ample foreshadowing. In such stories the interest is not in *what* will happen but in *how* it will happen.

Another way to put the matter is to say that foreshadowing makes a climax and denouement seem inevitable, as though this is the way the story *must* turn out. As we read we may not always be aware that a particular speech or action is functioning as foreshadowing, but it will have done its work if, later, we regard the denouement as inevitable.

Setting

When we begin to read a story and enter imaginatively into the world it presents, we need to get our bearings, that is, to find out where we are and, in general, what time it is. In telling us these things the author is providing the *setting* of the story by placing the action in space and time. Furthermore, in creating a well-drawn setting, he helps make his fictional world real to our imaginations, and consequently predisposes us to accept as plausible what happens in it. To see in particular how setting does this, we can consider some of the functions it performs, recognizing that it may perform more than one at a time. One important function—its use in portraying character—we have already touched on, under "Characterization by Externals."

SETTING AND PLOT

In many stories, what happens is so closely related to the setting that we can virtually say the actions are determined by it. This is true in stories of "travel": the River affects the actions of Huck Finn, the Oklahoma dust bowl affects the actions of the Joads in *The Grapes of Wrath*. This is equally true in Defoe's *Robinson Crusoe* and other stories of fixed locale. Conflict in *The Return of the Native* springs from the fact of Egdon Heath and what it means for people who live on it. The same could be said of the plains in the Nebraska novels of Willa Cather. Although in all of these stories the setting is nature itself, setting as motive force is also found in stories of city life. Here, however, the motive force is not strictly the pictured scene so much as it is the social and economic forces implied in the scene. In the one case setting *is* a motive force; in the other it *suggests* it.

SETTING AND "ATMOSPHERE"

When we visit a strange city one of the strongest impressions we receive is the *feel* of the place, hard to define but unmistakably sensed, perhaps more keenly on our first acquaintance with the spot than later. Writers of fiction often try to capture and record this elusive quality of place, which we call by the metaphoric term "atmosphere" to suggest its pervasiveness. Atmosphere can permeate a story so thoroughly as to give it its essential nature, which is why some students of fiction speak of the "atmosphere story" as though it were a special type of story. Used most effectively, atmosphere is not an end in itself but is a quality of setting that affects the characters. *They* feel it and are prompted by it to act, and the reader feels it, through sympathy with them as well as through the author's description. A classic example is Poe's "The Fall of the House of Usher."

Probably no analysis can isolate the secret of effective fictional atmosphere, its power over our emotions. Often it appears to be principally a matter of the selection of detail; rejecting much, the author presents details of setting that contribute to establishing a single, dominant atmosphere. It is this unity of impression that often enables us to sum up the pervasive atmosphere of a story in a single word or phrase: decay (of house, family, and mind) in "The Fall of the House of Usher"; wild passion (suggested by the Yorkshire moors) in *Wuthering Heights;* drowsiness in any of several of Mark Twain's descriptions of small river towns. Sometimes the atmosphere is too complex to be conveyed in a single word, or even in two or three. Although the reader of Henry James's *The Ambassadors,* imaginatively in sympathy with Lambert Strether, feels the unity of all the details that contribute to the atmosphere of Paris in that book, he would hesitate to say that "splendor," "cultivation," or "freedom" fully described that atmosphere.

SETTING AND IDEAS

Besides appealing to our senses and affecting our emotions, setting can also suggest ideas.

For the past hundred years men have become increasingly concerned with the question of man's relation to environment. At bottom it is a philosophical question, related to the age-old dispute about free will: does man determine his own destiny from within himself, or is his destiny determined for him by forces lying outside himself—that is, by his environment? Writers who hold the latter view may present setting as a determining force. In Stephen Crane's "The Open Boat," for example, a story of four men trying to reach land in a dinghy after a shipwreck, the setting of the sea is clearly involved with the actions of the men, and it provides a distinct emotional atmosphere, but it also does more. The sea (and, by extension, all of nature) is shown to be a great impersonal force, infinitely superior to—and indifferent to—man and his little efforts. The setting, then, contains philosophical implications. The same is true of many social novels, including a number written in the 1930's, where setting includes the social and economic forces that shape the lives of the characters.

Setting can also convey ideas by serving as symbol. In Hemingway's *A Farewell to Arms,* for instance, the parts of the story concerned with the war take place on the plains, which are hot and dusty or, with the rains, muddy. After Frederick Henry leaves the war, he retires with Catherine to the mountains, where it is cool and dry, and the air is pure. The setting in each case suggests symbolically the feelings and attitudes of the hero—war, hate, cynicism, and death on the one hand, and life, love, and spiritual exaltation on the other. It is true that such conditions of weather and terrain are what one expects in the sections of Italy described in the novel. But to say this is not to deny that the descriptive details coincide with—and suggest in the imaginative shorthand we call symbolism—the rather complex ideas and attitudes of the central character. In short, setting can be both realistic *and* symbolic.

Point of View

Earlier, considering character, we noted that a writer does not arbitrarily choose methods of revealing character, but rather selects the method or methods in keeping with his chosen *point of view*. By the point of view of a story (sometimes called "angle" or "focus" of narration), we mean the narrator's relation to the fictional world of the story and to the minds of the characters in it. When we read fiction we tacitly agree to a contract with the author: we agree to be willing to accept as imaginatively true what he tells us. We agree to do this, but we also expect the author to keep to the terms of the bargain—terms he himself sets when he begins to tell his story. They are two: (1) he must make clear to us where he, as narrator, stands in relation to the substance of the story; and (2) he must make clear which, if any, of the minds of his characters he presumes to be able to penetrate, and hence to reveal.

Let us put the matter another way. Assume a triangle situation involving Al, Bob, and Cathy, an emotional difficulty of some sort, the details of which we need not specify. Who could tell their story? Where would the narrator stand in relation to the story? What exactly could he divulge in the telling? The answers to these questions constitute the four main points of view in fiction.

1. Al could tell the story (or Bob or Cathy could tell it, though in each case it would be a different story) with himself as one of the characters; he would write in the first person and would probably tell us what he, but nobody else, thought and felt. He would be inside the story. An important variation on this method would be to have someone other than one of the principals—perhaps a parent or a friend—tell it. He too would write in the first person and would be inside the story, but he could not penetrate the minds of the principals. The point of view in both cases is usually called that of the *first person narrator*.

2. The narrator could be someone outside the story, who would speak of the principals as "he" and "she." If he wanted to focus on one of the

principals, say Al, he would take the liberty of assuming to know what Al thought and felt, and he would proceed to tell us. He would reveal what Cathy and Bob said and did, but he would not presume to read their minds, and so we would get only an indirect revelation of them. We would say that the narrator pretends he knows all—is omniscient—but chooses to reveal only a limited part of what he knows: the workings of Al's mind. This method is known as the *limited omniscient* point of view.

3. The narrator, again outside the story, could penetrate and reveal the minds of all three of the principals. In this case he would presume to know all and would take the liberty of telling all. We call this the *omniscient* point of view.

4. Finally, the narrator might choose to reveal none of the three minds. From outside the story he would report simply what the three people did (singly, in various pairs, or three together) and what they said (in various pairs, or all together). The story would resemble a play in that the narrator would be revealing things indirectly, through speech and action. At no point could he make a statement like "Cathy felt miserable," although he might report her appearance and say, "Cathy looked as though she felt miserable." Because all personal thoughts and feelings—subjective matters—are ruled out by this method, it is called the *objective* point of view.

The above discussion of these four points of view can be summed up in the following diagram. In each of the four cases the large circle represents the fictional world of the story; the small circles (*A, B, C*) represent the principal characters; *N* represents the narrator; each line connecting narrator to character either enters the circle of character or stops short of it, representing, respectively, the narrator's assumed right to enter a character's mind or his agreement not to.

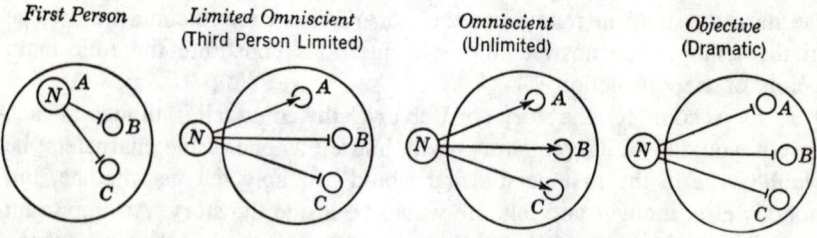

First Person	Limited Omniscient (Third Person Limited)	Omniscient (Unlimited)	Objective (Dramatic)

Each of these points of view has technical advantages, as well as disadvantages, which the others lack. A story told in the first person is likely to be convincing because the method of narration is a natural one; as in life, a person tells us directly what happened to him. It also seems more intimate than a story in the third person, and so we find it easier to identify ourselves with the central character, the "I" of the story. On the other hand, action is largely limited to what the narrator himself witnesses or takes part in. Also, when the main character and narrator are one, possibilities for analyzing the mind of the character will be limited if he is unperceptive or reticent, or both.

The other points of view also have advantages and disadvantages. The omniscient point of view, which reveals all minds, makes for subjective richness, but it may be that this value is achieved at the expense of selection and concentration. When such emphasis is desirable, the limited omniscient point of view may be used. Finally, the objective point of view in a way is the most lifelike, since its limitaton to action enables the narrator to present a scene in the way we would encounter it in life. We may, however, miss the analysis and wish the author had included some—had, that is, written from a different point of view. Or, we may like the subtlety of the objective method, the rich implication it permits, and the corresponding inference it requires from the reader.

POINT OF VIEW IN A POE STORY

We could generalize further about the several points of view, but it is doubtful that more generalization would be useful. One is on surer ground when he thinks of point of view in relation to a particular story. Consider Poe's "The Fall of the House of Usher." A man visits the house of his friend Roderick Usher, whom he has not seen for years, and whom he finds unkempt, melancholy, and unstable. Presumably Usher has degenerated through concern for the health of his twin sister, Madeline, who lives with him. When she "was no more," Usher, fearing a body-snatching physician might exhume her body to study her "strange malady," entombs her temporarily in a vault below. Later, at the height of a storm, with Usher reading aloud wildly from a book, Madeline appears, blood-stained from her struggle to escape. She falls dead, as does Usher, and as the visitor leaves, the house splits asunder and sinks into the "dank tarn." Here is the opening sentence:

During the whole of a dull, dark, and soundless day in the autumn of the year, when the clouds hung oppressively low in the heavens, I had been passing alone, on horseback, through a singularly dreary tract of country; and at length found myself, as the shades of the evening drew on, within view of the melancholy House of Usher.

We notice at once that the narrator, the visitor, is within the story and so tells it in the first person. It is apparent, if we think about it, that Poe has chosen quite the best point of view from which to tell his story. One way to test this judgment is to ask what the story would have been like told from other points of view.

From the objective point of view all would have to be told through narrative and description. The visitor's speculations about Usher and Madeline as well as his statements of his own feelings would be ruled out. This would be a decided loss, since these elements do much to enhance the eerie effect of the scene.

If analysis of minds is valuable, then, what about using the omniscient point of view? Clearly, the author would not want, *for the purpose of this story,* to enter the minds of Usher and Madeline; these are a mystery and must remain so. What about limited omniscient? The point of view could not be limited to either Usher or Madeline, for the reason just stated. (Conceivably quite a story could be written from Madeline's point of view, but it would be a totally different affair.) That leaves the visitor as a possibility, and since we know his mind in the story as it stands, the only question is this: Is it better to reveal the visitor in the third or in the first person?

Either the third or the first person would do what is needed for the story, namely, to have a sensitive register of events—a consciousness that reacts, that *feels* what is happening. This consciousness is better presented in the first person, however, for the reasons stated above as advantages of this point of view, particularly the advantage of intimacy. For Poe unquestionably wanted to stir the reader as well as his narrator-visitor, and apparently he felt he could do this by showing the visitor becoming progressively terrified, and by using the point of view that would identify the reader most closely with him. The reader, too, then, would become progressively terrified. In another connection Poe spoke of showing a change of thought in a character so as "to induce a similar one on the part of the reader." In the present story the visitor exhibits a change not of thought but of feeling; calm and dispassionate at the start, he is nearly mad himself when the story ends. As readers we feel this change in him, and we feel it so acutely because, *largely as a result of the first person point of view,* we have identified ourselves with him.

This, then, is one way to inquire into the significance of a story's point of view. It should be clear from our discussion of the Poe story that a point of view is neither "good" nor "bad" in any absolute sense; one is better than another insofar as it is more appropriate to the particular story the author has to tell. Each of the four points of view has its advantages and disadvantages. Realizing this, a writer usually selects and maintains his point of view with great care. As readers we, too, should be attentive to it, for it plays an important part in giving to a piece of fiction its emphasis, direction, and focus.

Meaning in Fiction

The interrelatedness of fictional elements, which we have been assuming all along, certainly extends to the ideas, or intellectual content, of a story. But just as we have isolated the elements of character, plot, setting, and point of view, in order to talk about them, so can we isolate the ideas of fiction to see the part they play in a work.

THEME IN FICTION

In discussing a story we often find it convenient to speak of its *theme*. The theme is what the story is essentially "about"—not the subject matter, but the essential significance of the subject matter and the author's conception of it. Theme may be of central importance in a story, as in one of Aesop's fables, or in Mark Twain's "The Man That Corrupted Hadleyburg"; often it figures less prominently. It may be stated explicitly, as in many of Hawthorne's stories; more commonly it is only implied, requiring the reader to infer it. This is a process of abstraction. A story is composed of particular actions embodying a central significance. In *Huckleberry Finn* most of the actions involve Huck's and Jim's efforts to escape from people who repress them. Abstracted, these actions could be summed up in the phrase "freedom *vs.* social restraint," and this we would call the theme.

Theme, best stated as a noun or noun phrase rather than as a complete sentence, is the core of meaning in a story. We can isolate it in order to discuss it and to see how it functions. But we should realize that theme is never *the* meaning of a story. A story's meaning is nothing less than the sum total of all fictional elements, harmoniously interrelated in an artistic whole. Henry James thought of fiction in this way when in his essay "The Art of Fiction" he offered advice to young writers. "Do not think too much about optimism and pessimism; try and catch the color of life itself." If a writer proceeds in this way, James suggests, the doctrinal content, the "ideas," will not obtrude but will be properly integrated in the whole. They will be implied in character and action, from which the reader may derive them.

DERIVING THE AUTHOR'S OPINION

In fiction in which ideas stand out prominently or in which an omniscient author comments in explanatory essay fashion, it is no problem to determine the author's opinion. But when ideas are embodied in the story itself, how do we tell what the author believes?

We learn something by noting his characters. It is a mistake to assume that a character is *necessarily* voicing the author's views; often we feel that he is, but we should be slow to come to this conclusion. A safer procedure is to notice how the author feels about a character as seen in the way he presents him. If he presents him in approving terms so that we find him attractive, the character is likely to represent what the author believes. There are many exceptions to this principle; some writers take pains *not* to choose sides. But when the author does take sides, probably the sympathetic characters come closer than the others to representing his opinions. The converse is also true. Mark Twain makes Huck's father such a repellent character that we feel certain the author's opinions on the Negro and on government are quite different from those voiced by Pap Finn.

Perhaps even more reliable clues to the ideas of an author are the nature of the conflict he presents and the way he resolves it. In Stephen Crane's *The Red Badge of Courage* a young man caught up in the excitement of the Civil War enlists in the Union Army, hoping to become a hero by valorous acts. Under fire for the first time, he runs, is accidentally hit on the head, and turns up among the wounded. He becomes a hero, but in a way quite different from what he anticipated. Although the author makes few direct philosophical statements about the determining causes in life, we can deduce that Crane believes in what we might call the irony of fate. We determine his view not by noting what he or a character says, but by noting the boy's conflict and the way it is resolved.

Our guesses about an author's basic ideas can often be confirmed by reading several of his works. Hemingway's idea of the virtue of man's bravely facing death alone, Faulkner's idea of slavery's lying like a curse on the South, Hardy's view of the active role of chance in human affairs —these ideas are found, respectively, in several of these writers' works. But whether we consider one or several of a man's books, we can deduce a great deal about his opinions as to how the world operates by noting the terms of the conflicts his characters are involved in, and how those conflicts are worked out.

MORALITY IN FICTION

"Moral" is a word we apply in life to conduct or character when we judge them in terms of good and bad, right and wrong; we use it in a similar way in speaking of fictional personages and their actions. The sum total of moral behavior of the characters, together with stated or implied relevant comment of the author, we speak of broadly as the book's "moral content." Readers react differently to the presence of moral content in a book. For the purpose of discussion let us consider two polar extremes —those readers who strongly approve its presence, and those, a smaller number, who disapprove.

Many readers judge a novel largely on the basis of its moral content. If the book shows admirable people behaving admirably, it is a good book; if it shows people behaving in an ugly, evil way, it is a bad book— particularly if the behavior is represented vividly and in language that is "bad," that is, socially unacceptable. Such a view of fiction is decidedly narrow, although there may be practical considerations, such as selecting books for younger readers, that sometimes make this criterion necessary.

At the other extreme are readers who are impatient with the moral element. Possibly in reaction against the moral criterion of fiction, they argue that a novel is a work of art, and that consequently it should not be concerned with morality. When it is, they feel it is *didactic,* that is, designed to teach a lesson, and they will use the merely descriptive term "didactic" as a term of disapproval. This view of fiction, as it stands, is also narrow. People who hold it make two errors: (1) they construe the word "moral" too narrowly, and (2) they confuse "moral content" with *obtrusiveness* of moral content. Let us consider these errors separately.

We often use the term "moral" to describe the conduct of a person who avoids the grosser forms of evil. If he avoids committing murder or swindling his associates, above all if he avoids a life of sexual profligacy, we are likely to say he is moral; at least if he does *not* avoid them we are likely to call him immoral. But a moment's thought tells us that morality is broader than this. In a sense, all choices are moral ones. We need not push the matter so far, however, to recognize that morality extends beyond that which is clearly and admittedly moral. Consider Sinclair Lewis's Babbitt. On the whole he behaves himself pretty well, but he is an overgrown boy, an immature, back-slapping fellow who shirks his responsibilities—to his job as real-estate man, to his city, to his family, and to himself. Although his conduct is like that of many people, and although it is treated humorously, it nonetheless can be said to be somewhat immoral. If we understand "moral" in this broader sense, therefore, we would have to agree that a great deal of fiction, perhaps most of it, is moral.

Some older writers in both prose and verse were inclined to emphasize the moral content of their work, even, as it were, to the point of underlining it. Today this practice is legitimately resented by discriminating readers. A work of literary art, they feel, should be a harmonious whole, and the harmony is damaged if the moral content obtrudes. Moreover, obtrusive moral content is unlifelike. In life such matter is firmly embedded in actions, and we feel that in a story, too, morality should be an inherent part of the action, rather than a preachment that we can label "the moral" of the story.

Fiction in which the moral content obtrudes often has a relatively short life. It may do its work as propaganda, but when the issues it debates are dead, the book is likely to die also. This has happened to Harriet Beecher Stowe's *Uncle Tom's Cabin,* although it will long live as a historical document. Perhaps it is too soon to say whether the same fate will befall *The Grapes of Wrath,* but one suspects that it will not. There is preachment in Steinbeck's novel. The moral content, however, is more an exploration of a problem than a suggested solution. Also, although it clearly involves the plight of people living at a certain time in a certain place, it has universal relevance in its portrayal of oppression of the weak by the strong. Finally, and most importantly, the preachment is inherent in the natures and actions of very believable characters, the Joads. When moral content is an integral part of a well-told story, as is true in the best of the world's fiction, we value it highly as an enrichment of the story.

THE SHORT STORY

Prose fiction is often classified as to length: the novel, the short novel, the novelette (French term, "nouvelle"), the long short story, the short story, and the short short story. Although they overlap, these terms are useful. But it would be misleading to think that a short story is simply a piece of prose fiction that is short, a sort of condensed novel. For the short story has aims, features, and qualities of its own, which distinguish it significantly, in terms besides length, from other prose fiction.

Much of what needs to be said about the short story has already been touched on in our discussion of the elements of prose fiction. These elements are found in the short story as well as in the novel. In the short story, however, they are handled in a way peculiar to this form of fiction. What determines the handling is the *shortness* of the story. *Plot* is often minimized; in its place is a situation, and the interest of the story lies in the way characters react to it. *Character* must be presented economically. Only those traits are mentioned which are relevant to the situation, and even these are not revealed separately but are inherent in the action. *Setting* is also treated economically. A few well-chosen details can lay the scene, reveal character, and indicate the situation. A definite *point of view* is strictly maintained. *Ideas* may be present, but are usually inherent in character, situation, and action. *Language* is used for maximum effect. Every word counts. Charged with suggestiveness, the language has some of the evocative power, as well as the compression, of poetry.

Most of these qualities of the short story were noted by Edgar Allan Poe in what has come to be regarded as one of the classic definitions of the short story:

[Since the ordinary novel] cannot be read at one sitting, it deprives itself, of course, of the immense force derivable from *totality*. Worldly interests intervening during the pauses of perusal, modify, annul, or counteract, in a greater or less degree, the impressions of the book. But simple cessation in reading would, of itself, be sufficient to destroy the true unity. In the brief tale, however, the author is enabled to carry out the fulness of his intention, be it what it may. . . .

A skilful literary artist has constructed a tale. If wise, he has not fashioned his thoughts to accommodate his incidents; but having conceived, with deliberate :are, a certain unique or single *effect* to be wrought out, he then invents such ncidents—he then combines such events as may best aid him in establishing this preconceived effect. If his very initial sentence tend not to the outbringing of this effect, then he has failed in his first step. In the whole composition there should be no word written, of which the tendency, direct or indirect, is not to the one preëstablished design. And by such means, with such care and skill, a picture is at length painted which leaves in the mind of him who contemplates it with a kindred art, a sense of the fullest satisfaction. The idea of the tale has been presented unblemished, because undisturbed; and this is an end unattainable by the novel. Undue brevity is just as exceptionable here as in the poem; but undue length is yet more to be avoided.[1]

The salient qualities are here. Because of its *brevity* the short story requires *selectivity* of detail (and hence *economy* and *emphasis*), and this makes possible the all-important quality of *unity* ("totality," "single *effect*"). Poe also notes the crucial role of language when he says "there should be no word written" that does not contribute to the "preëstablished design." One might think Poe an unduly mechanical theorist, his "preëstablished design" suggesting a kind of blueprint which a writer follows mechanically. His doctrine is sound, however, for it is hard to see how in brief compass a writer could achieve unity through selectivity *without* a preëstablished design. The very nature of the short story demands conscious artistry.

A poet who had been explaining one of his intricate poems was asked how much time he expected a reader to spend studying his poem. His reply: As much time as it took me to write it. This is an extreme statement of a principle essentially sound. For writing that is tightly packed with meaning and rich in suggestion cannot be read superficially; art has gone into its creation, and its values will be fully revealed, Poe says, only to "him who contemplates it with a kindred art." More than any other literary form except poetry, the short story demands of the reader an intellectual and imaginative alertness, a capacity and a willingness to make inferences from what little data the author presents.

For Further Reading

Brooks, Cleanth, and Robert Penn Warren. *Understanding Fiction*. New York: Appleton-Century-Crofts, 1943.

Forster, E. M. *Aspects of the Novel*. New York: Harcourt, Brace, 1927. (Harvest Books)

Millett, Fred B. *Reading Fiction*. New York: Harper, 1950.

Lubbock, Percy. *The Craft of Fiction*. New York: Viking, 1947. (Compass Books)

O'Faolain, Sean. *The Short Story*. New York: Devin-Adair, 1951.

[1] From Poe's review (1842) of Hawthorne's *Twice-Told Tales*.

• III •

DRAMA

THE NATURE OF DRAMA

Of the three major forms of imaginative literature—fiction, drama, and poetry—it is drama with which students are most familiar. Nearly everyone has seen scores of movies and television plays. To study the workings of the drama might increase one's enjoyment of these forms of entertainment, but they are addressed to people without special training, and in a sense the viewer needs none. Quite different, however, are plays that have continued to entertain and move men for hundreds of years, as well as serious modern plays. These are properly regarded as literature of the highest order. Like poetry and fiction, the drama has its own principles, and it is these with which the present chapter is concerned.

Although we use the word "dramatic" generally in the sense of "startling," "vivid," or "exciting," it is not essentially these qualities we have in mind when we speak of the dramatic quality of a play. One essential ingredient in drama is *conflict*. The conflict may take any one of several forms: a wrong to be righted, a misunderstanding to be cleared up, a problem to be solved, a moral dilemma to be resolved, an enemy to be overcome, a woman to be won—all of which involve a character facing choices and making decisions, that is, taking *action* of some sort. Action, too, then, is necessary. It may be physical action (we are not speaking of the casual lighting of a cigarette, or thumbing of a magazine—the "business" that adds naturalness to a scene), or it may be mental action, like accepting a proposal or cutting off an heir in a will. Such action will be rendered in speech, but it is speech that gets somewhere, that contributes to the development or settlement of the conflict. Talk by itself is not enough; it must advance the action.

This requirement, as well as several others, results from the conditions that are peculiar to a play and so distinguish it from fiction. A play is written to be acted, not told. Its point of view is necessarily objective (see "Point of View," in Chapter II). It must be presented in a limited time, usually under three hours. It normally appeals to a wide audience, and the assumption is that it will not, like a story, be re-examined; rather, it is a "one-shot" performance. These conditions impose restrictions on the drama. But they also afford opportunities that give the drama its essential nature. To see this in some detail, let us consider some of the elements common to fiction and drama, and notice how they function in a play.

THE ELEMENTS OF DRAMA

Plot

A play, like fiction, makes a progress from beginning, through middle, to end—or from exposition, through complication, to resolution or denouement. But the nature of drama requires the progress to be more rapid and freer of interruptions than it often is in fiction. Also, it is usually clearer. Divisions into act and scene, serving to block out the action in functional units, allow us to pause and take stock of the situation, that is, to look back and forward to see where the characters stand in relation to the problem they face.

The exposition performs several functions at once. It sets the action in time and place, it makes us acquainted with the characters, it reveals the situation they are in, it initiates the conflict to be developed, and it may introduce foreshadowing to hint at the resolution and so make it plausible when it occurs. All these things must be done clearly and definitely, both because an observer (or reader), not yet engrossed in the play, is likely to be less attentive than he will be later on, and because our understanding of what follows depends on them. They must also be done quickly. Too much exposition kills interest; an audience is impatient to "get on with the show." For these reasons many a playwright has found his first act the hardest to write.

The complication, or middle part of the play, develops the conflict initiated by the exposition. Between the *protagonist* (the hero, or central character) and his goal are placed obstacles which he must overcome; misunderstandings are generated; problems or questions are debated. More leisurely than either the exposition or the denouement, this central portion of the play enables us to get to know the characters more thoroughly. Sometimes it provides "flashbacks" into the lives of the characters at a period previous to the time covered by the play. Such flashbacks (which the exposition, moving rapidly, usually cannot afford to include) serve to enrich character, to clarify the situation and the nature of the conflict, and often to provide motivation.

Motivation is always important in a play. As we do in fiction, so in a play we expect characters to act "in character," that is, to do what an audience, on the basis of what it knows about them, can legitimately expect them to do. A playwright usually sees to it, however, that distinct motives, or reasons for actions, are made clear. He will take special pains to insert motivations for a character who undergoes a marked change in the course of the play. He must do this because the relatively short time it takes us to read or see the play, even if we are told in the directions that "a month has passed," tends to make fundamental changes of heart or mind implausible. A compensation for this disadvantage of the restricted time of a play, however, is the magic of the theater. When a play is well produced, it can make actions plausible which, on close scrutiny, we might reject as implausible. Shakespeare's *Othello* is a celebrated instance. Although some readers of the play feel that Iago's diabolical actions in arousing Othello's jealousy are adequately motivated, many do not. Even these readers, however, usually feel that in spite of the inadequate motivation of Iago's actions, these actions are made to *seem* probable.

A related kind of probability has to do with actions that do not stem essentially from the characters. (See "Probability of Actions," under "Plot" in Chapter II.) Perhaps in serious drama, at least, more than in fiction we are quick to resent what we sometimes call "unmotivated" events—not only accidents, but happenings that appear to be introduced merely to make the plot come out right: a rich relative dies and leaves an inheritance to the perplexed hero, thus solving his problems. Such an event is often called a *deus ex machina* (literally, "god from the machine"), from the practice in Greek drama of actually lowering from above, in a basket, an actor impersonating a god, who resolved the tangled plot.

Ideally the denouement arises logically from what has preceded it in the complication. The point separating these two main parts (separating what is sometimes called the "rising action" from the "falling action") is usually called the *climax,* or turning point, or reversal. It is the point which marks the crucial shift in the character's fortunes, or, to put it another way, the point at which it becomes quite apparent what direction the plot will take. Some critics prefer to call this point the *crisis* of the play, reserving the term "climax" for the point of greatest emotional interest. Our satisfaction in the denouement follows from our realizing that things are turning out as we have been led to expect they would: sometimes happily, perhaps with *poetic justice* being served—the good rewarded, the evil punished—and sometimes tragically, but always, in the best plays, inevitably.

A play that tells a single story through a well-knit plot, that is, a plot composed of events logically related and strictly relevant to the main concern, we say has unity of action. Ever since it was first mentioned by Aristotle, this dramatic ideal has been honored by playwrights, but not by all of them. The Elizabethan dramatists, for instance, liked to introduce subordinate lines of action in a play, to provide variety and hence to widen the play's appeal. Such a subplot may be so remote from the central action as to mar the play's unity. But when a subplot provides a structural or thematic parallel to the main action, we feel that variety is achieved without real loss of unity. Instances in Shakespeare are the Falstaff plot in *Henry IV Part I,* the Caliban-Stephano-Trinculo plot in *The Tempest,* and the Gloucester plot in *King Lear.*

Setting

Another way a dramatist can give unity to a play is to represent the action as occurring at a single place and at a single time. The desirability of such unity so impressed earlier students of the drama that they built a theory around it, which has had considerable influence on later playwrights. As we have seen, Aristotle felt that unity of action was indispensable to a play. Also, drawing on the actual practice of the Greek theater, as he does throughout the dramatic portions of the *Poetics,* he observed that tragedy usually was confined to "a single revolution of the sun," but he did not insist that such a restriction of time was essential. Italian and French critics of the sixteenth and seventeenth centuries, however, made of his comment on time a rigid and absolute principle of dramatic construction. In addition, they argued that if the action were confined to one day, it most likely would be confined also to one place, a matter that Aristotle had not mentioned at all. In this way arose the neoclassic concept of the *dramatic unities*—of action, time, and place.

The three unities were scrupulously observed by many playwrights in the seventeenth and early eighteenth centuries—Molière and Racine in France, Congreve and Dryden in England are examples—who thereby achieved admirable compression and emphasis in their plays. But desirable as these qualities are, they may be dearly bought. Unity of construction alone does not make a play great, as a comparison of two dramatic treatments of Antony and Cleopatra shows: Dryden's *All for Love* carefully observes the unities, but it lacks the sweep, the grandeur, and the exotic appeal of Shakespeare's *Antony and Cleopatra*. Furthermore, neglect of the three unities does not necessarily mean the loss of all unity. Unity of action is indispensable, it is true, but the other two are not; ignoring them, one can still achieve unity through such elements as theme and atmosphere.

Assuming that the action of a play is restricted to one place, what can setting do for a play? It can economically reveal character, it can influence the actions of characters, it can provide atmosphere, and it can suggest ideas. Since these functions have been discussed in connection with fiction (see "Setting," under "The Elements of Fiction" in Chapter II), we need not consider them again. It should be remembered, of course, that what the writer of fiction describes in words is portrayed on a stage with actual objects or representations of objects—a notable economy for the dramatist, since a glance takes in the stage set. Because a set can do so much for a play, a producer will often devote much care and money to its creation. On the other hand, it is possible for a set to be too elaborate, and so to detract from other elements in the play. Some modern producers of Shakespeare prefer to keep their sets simple and unobtrusive so that attention is focused on the characters and their delivery of Shakespeare's words.

Character

Much that was said in the preceding chapter about character in fiction applies equally well to the drama. It may be useful, however, to reconsider some of these matters to see their role in drama in particular.

KINDS OF CHARACTERS

Although several of the following kinds of characters are found in both fiction and drama, they are probably commoner in the latter because they are so well suited to essential features of the drama: its brevity and the fact that it is presented directly before an audience. As we have seen, the relative brevity of a play means that impressions must be made quickly and clearly. Also, the performance of a play is a *projection* of a story to the audience. Just as an actor does not speak in natural conversational tones, but rather heightens and modifies his inflections and intonations in order to "get across" to an audience, so is the whole play, text as well as performance, designed to get across clearly.

1. One kind of character that helps dramatic projection is a *foil,* or a character who, standing in contrast to another character, helps to define him. He may be a minor character, whose only function is to serve as a foil; or he may play a major part in the action and serve as foil somewhat incidentally. In Shakespeare's *Henry IV Part I,* Hotspur and Prince Hal are foils to each other.

2. The *type* character is also used because he can be quickly and clearly portrayed. He is representative of a country, an occupation, a manner of life—the excitable Frenchman, the stern upholder of justice in Westerns, the vacuous clubwoman, and lately on television, the bungling father. (When such characters are not only representative of a recognizable group in life but recur in play after play, they are also called *stock* characters.) The fact that we speak of "the" rather than "a" Western lawman shows that we consider him a type. Probably because they are dramatically economical, type characters have been widely used since the days of Roman comedy. In Shakespeare's day Ben Jonson built plays around psychological types, each of whom was motivated by one dominant trait, or "humor," in his constitution. Jonson gave such characters names frankly indicative of their type nature—Sir Epicure Mammon, a voluptuary; Volpone (fox), a shrewd schemer; Zeal-of-the-land Busy, a Puritan—and for years dramatists followed his practice.

The prevalence of type characters in the drama and their suitability to the needs of the dramatic medium make it all the more remarkable when a truly individual character is created. We should realize, however, that what we call individuality in characterization is not uniqueness (we would not recognize a character altogether unique), but rather a combination of well-known, even "type," traits. It has been shown, for instance, that Shakespeare's Falstaff combines traits of three well-known dramatic types: the boastful soldier, the alehouse jester, and the parasite. Even Hamlet, one of the most individual characters in all literature, has been shown to embody the traits of the melancholy man and the hero dedicated to revenge, both of which were familiar dramatic types. What gives both of these characters individuality is the new combination of old ingredients, plus, of course, the fact that their creator blew the breath of life into them.

3. A play tends to show *static* rather than *developing* characters, again because of the limited time at its disposal. Circumstances may make the actions of a character at the end of the play different from what they were at the beginning, but usually his basic nature will be the same throughout. Here, too, we find an exception in Shakespeare, who was able to overcome seemingly insurmountable obstacles, and triumphantly. Othello changes from a stable, dignified, affectionate man at the outset of the play, to a man of violent passion at the end. It is quite possible that Shakespeare chose a Moor for the role of the jealous husband because to the Elizabethans a Moor was a type character, generally accepted as being passionate and cruel. Shakespeare could count on this general opinion to strengthen the probability of the quick change in Othello's character.

The development of Macbeth's character is even more remarkable. Macbeth is first shown returning from an engagement in which he has put down rebels against his king; before long, his ambition stirred by the witches' prophecy and encouraged by his wife, he murders his king—certainly a quick change from loyalty to extreme disloyalty. Yet it is quite plausible. It will not do to argue that the change is plausible because all men have the seeds of evil implanted in them. Indeed they do, but when the seeds grow, as a rule they grow slowly. One could learn a good deal by inquiring how Shakespeare was able to make such a rapid degeneration believable. The supernatural witches figure in this matter, and so does Lady Macbeth. The point at the moment, however, is that although many novelists have successfully pictured degeneration, most playwrights have found the problem too difficult for the drama and have been content to use static characters.

REVELATION OF CHARACTER

Our previous discussion of how character is revealed in fiction applies, with few modifications, to drama as well. Perhaps it is worth noting that the first four methods of character revelation discussed in Chapter II are listed in the order in which we usually encounter them in watching a play. Often the appearance of the central character is deferred while subordinate characters prepare for his appearance by talking about him. (In Molière's *Tartuffe,* an extreme case, the minor characters talk about Tartuffe for two acts before he appears in the third of the five acts.) The central character then appears and is characterized by physical appearance and by speech and action. Characterization "by the author's statement" obviously is impossible in a play. What of the sixth method, revealing a character's thoughts? Here fiction has an advantage over the drama, which has always found this a knotty problem. A character in a play can speak his thoughts to other characters, but with many of them he may be in conflict, as in *Hamlet,* and so will not say what he truly thinks.

Dramatists have solved this difficulty in several ways. One way, used also in fiction, involves the use of a *confidant,* a character who is sympathetic with the main character and who "draws him out." When he is a mere sounding board, he serves only a mechanical function in the play and his presence is likely to strike us as clumsy workmanship. Shakespeare, however, with his genius for using the ordinary device (or plot, or theme, or character, or form) but managing to transcend it, makes of Horatio, Hamlet's confidant, an interesting, likable character in his own right.

The *aside,* a device peculiar to drama, is another way a character can reveal his true thoughts. He turns aside and addresses the audience in a "stage whisper"; that is, he pretends to whisper so that the other characters will not hear him, but actually speaks loud enough to be heard throughout the audience. The patent artificiality of the aside has tended to make it unacceptable in realistic drama. Eugene O'Neill, however, used it all through *Strange Interlude* to indicate the discrepancy between what characters said and what they felt. The device is still used by the comedian who tosses a gag to the audience in the form of a pretended confidence, uttered behind the hand. In older plays, lines to be delivered as asides are preceded by the stage direction "aside."

Formerly the commonest way to reveal a character's thoughts in some fullness was through use of the *soliloquy*—a speech delivered by a character alone on the stage. The soliloquy had a good deal to recommend it. In using it, Shakepeare wrote some of the most superb poetry of all time. Furthermore, the soliloquy is not wholly implausible. People *do* talk to themselves; and besides, when an actor delivers a soliloquy, he does not appear to be establishing a confidential relationship with the audience (as is true with the aside), but simply to be thinking aloud, and to be quite unaware of an audience. Nevertheless, with the development of realism in the drama, the soliloquy, like the aside, has tended to disappear. Something like it is still seen in some films and television shows. We see a character, writing a letter or in an attitude of reflection, and we hear what purports to be his voice; but because his lips do not move, we are to believe he is not speaking the statements but thinking them. This device tries to reap the advantages of the soliloquy without violating the canons of realism.

All three of these devices for portraying subjective matter—the confidant, the aside, and the soliloquy—reveal the drama struggling to escape the restrictions of objectivity that are inherent in the dramatic medium. Our quarrel with the devices—except, of course, in older plays—is not so much that they are unrealistic. If one is willing to accept the convention of a stage or, indeed, of acting itself, he should not find it hard to go one step further in imagination and to accept these subjective devices. A more legitimate objection is that the drama, being by nature an objective medium, is not entitled to present subjectivity except implicitly. When it attempts analysis, as in the soliloquy, it begins to encroach on the realm of fiction.

Dialogue

Although it is true in theory that dialogue is not indispensable to drama—witness the early films of Charlie Chaplin, in which no word was spoken—normally it is a major ingredient. In fiction it is one of several ways of telling the story; in plays it is the only way. What is required of it?

For one thing, dialogue must advance the action. It is not hard to put characters together and make them talk, and talk interestingly, but the dramatist must do more. He must see to it that the talk leads somewhere. It reveals what has happened before the period of time represented by the play, it reveals what is happening during that period but happening offstage, and it reveals the thoughts and feelings of the characters on the stage. On the basis of this information a character will act or will suffer a change of heart or mind that promises future action.

In talking, the characters reveal themselves, as we have seen. The speech of the several characters, therefore, must be sharply distinguished so that we can clearly infer their character from what they say and how they say it. An inexperienced reader may encounter difficulty here in reading older dramatists; because Elizabethan English, for instance, strikes him as strange and remote, he may find it hard to recognize differences in the way the several characters speak. All that is needed, though, is a little careful reading, for the differences in the speech habits of the characters in, say, Shakespeare's *Henry IV Part I* are quite marked. Indeed, one could make an interesting character study of the leading figures in that play simply on the basis of the way they speak.

We sometimes say that, to be convincing, the speech of characters should be "natural," or lifelike, but the term is of questionable value. Until we are familiar with the English language in older periods we cannot tell what speech resembles speech in life and what does not. Furthermore, we need to remember that before the eighteenth century the usual language of drama was poetry, which by its nature is somewhat removed from everyday speech. Even the prose in more recent plays is something more than "natural" speech. Because a play is projected, as we noted above, the speech of the characters is carefully tailored to that end: characters speak lucidly and to the point, no words are wasted, witty characters are invariably witty, pompous ones invariably pompous—in short, all is heightened and exaggerated. It may *seem* natural, however, especially if the dramatist has caught the idiom and rhythm of actual speech. Dialogue has more to do than merely "sound right," but certainly speech that rings true does much to create a convincing illusion of life.

TYPES OF PLAYS

A knowledge of the technical elements in drama, which we have been considering, helps us to read or see a play intelligently. In addition to a knowledge of technique, we need to know something about the several classes or types of plays. Each type has its own principles, and if we do not know them, we cannot read a given play properly or judge it fairly. The two main types, universally recognized since the time of the Greeks, are tragedy and comedy. To these we can add the two related minor types, melodrama and farce.

Tragedy

The word "tragedy" was first used by the Greeks to describe a certain type of play. Because the protagonist in a tragedy met an unhappy end, usually death, the word came to be applied—by an understandable process of exaggeration—to a situation in life in which one suffered severe misfortune, often death. This is the sense of the word with which we are all familiar; death from an automobile accident, we say, is a tragedy. Legitimate as this common meaning is, it can confuse us in our thinking about the drama because it seems to suggest that death is what is central to a tragic drama, whereas other elements are really more important.

A tragedy is fundamentally a serious play. It presents a character in most ways admirable, who faces a moral issue; the issue is not peculiar to him but is one that any man might have to face—a universal issue. The forces of life being what they are, and human nature what it is, the protagonist will wrestle with these forces, but he cannot hope to win over them, and ultimately he is defeated. A play that engages our interest in such basic, serious questions must deal with us honestly. Character must be richly developed so as to be believable; our sympathy cannot be enlisted for a shadowy figure. There should not be many twists and turns of plot (one main reversal is common), for we need to concentrate on character in a single situation. Motive must be clear and adequate.

The single quality resulting from such technical features is inevitability. We must feel that the protagonist's fate is necessary, inexorable, not to be escaped. Our realization that the protagonist, thus caught, is the victim of a superior force arouses our pity; and our realization that the action demonstrates a universal truth and that therefore the victim could just as easily be ourselves—this arouses our fear. Tragedy arouses pity and fear, said Aristotle, but it also purges us of these feelings (his term is *catharsis*). The exact meaning of his statement has been much debated. It seems to refer to what many viewers of tragedy experience at the end of the play—not a sense of sadness and depression, but rather, oddly, one of elation. One hesitates to say why this should be so, but very likely it is because the protagonist, before his final defeat, has measured for us the value of human nature. In his death we feel a sense of loss, but only because he has demonstrated his great worth. The difference between tragedy in the popular sense and tragedy in drama should now be clear: in a dramatic tragedy the catastrophe is not accidental but inevitable; it is not a mere death, nor even necessarily an untimely one, but a death resulting only after great struggle against the forces of life; and its effect on observers is not one of sorrow and devastation, but of exaltation.

The nature of the tragic hero and the nature of the conflict he is engaged in have changed as man's ideas about himself and his world have changed. The Greek tragic hero is a man of high estate, of royal or noble position—Agamemnon, Oedipus, Orestes. He or his forebears have transgressed the moral law, embodied in the gods and the state, and the play shows him struggling to avoid the consequences of the transgression. He may err in thinking he can escape the consequences—may, that is, exhibit a fatal pride. His conflict, however, is with forces outside himself, and he is inevitably the loser in the struggle. The Elizabethan tragic hero is also an eminent man, but his conflict is usually within himself. Good, or at least grand, he nevertheless possesses a "tragic flaw," which is demonstrated in the play as leading to his downfall. In Marlowe's Faustus it is excessive intellectual ambition, in Macbeth it is excessive political ambition, in Hamlet it is perhaps an excessive moral and intellectual niceness.

Plays of the Norwegian dramatist Henrik Ibsen come as close as any in more modern times to fulfilling the requirements of tragedy. They are quite different from earlier tragedy. The hero is from the middle classes. His conflict, although it has broad moral implications, is usually of a domestic or social nature. Ibsen's plays, written in prose rather than verse, are often called "problem plays," since they are concerned primarily with exploring some of the personal and social problems of modern man. Many students of the drama feel that tragedy in the traditional sense is impossible in the modern world, and that the chief modern counterpart is the problem play.

Comedy

We usually think of a comedy as a play that is funny or, more technically, as one that has a happy ending. These features are found in most comedies but not in all. It is difficult to isolate any one feature common to all comedies because the term "comedy" is applied to so many different kinds of plays. About all one can say by way of generalization is that although comedy often pictures life accurately and with shrewd insight, it does not try to picture it profoundly. It will say, "See how amusing, how foolish, how illogical—or how warmhearted and decent—people are," but it does not go beyond this and try, as tragedy does, to say something basic and profound about the nature of man. Consequently we are likely to view comedy with more detachment, to be less deeply involved emotionally in the fate of the characters.

Certainly we view with detachment that comedy which satirizes or mocks human nature by holding its follies up to ridicule—the "humors" comedy of Ben Jonson (*The Alchemist*), Molière's comedy of character (*Tartuffe*), Restoration comedy of manners (Congreve's *The Way of the World*), or Bernard Shaw's satiric comedies (*Major Barbara*). Satire calls for detachment on the part of both playwright and audience, for it is a process of measuring, weighing, evaluating conduct in relation to some norm of behavior. In short, satiric comedy is intellectual rather than emotional, and the amusement it provides is likely to be wit rather than humor.

It is true that we become emotionally involved in some types of comedy. In Shakespeare's romantic comedy—for instance, *Twelfth Night, As You Like It*—we sympathize with the lovers and wish them well in their affairs of the heart. Likewise in the comedy of manners of the late eighteenth century (Goldsmith's *She Stoops to Conquer,* and Sheridan's *The Rivals* and *The School for Scandal*), we warm to the good-natured heroes and applaud their successes. The same is true, of course, with the countless love stories in modern plays and films. But however more emotionally involved we become in these plays than in more intellectual comedies, it is not the profound involvement that we experience with tragedy. This is not to say that comedy is inferior to tragedy, but simply that it is a different genre and so has a different tone. Each genre has its own kind of value and should be appreciated for what it is.

Melodrama and Farce

The term "tragedy" was formerly broad enough to include both truly serious plays dealing with moral struggles and those that only seemed to do so. Since about 1800 the term "melodrama" has been used to denote the latter. In melodrama, as in tragedy, the hero is engaged in a serious difficulty, often a life-and-death struggle. In melodrama he usually wins and in tragedy loses. Usually but not always, for the ending in each case is more a symptom or accompanying characteristic than an indispensable requirement. The situation of melodrama may closely resemble that of tragedy, and so may the characters and action, at least superficially. What distinguishes melodrama from tragedy is that it seeks to interest us in the action *for its own sake*. The action is exciting, full of thrills. We have no need for subtleties of character, or motive, or theme, all of which must be kept plain and simple to clear the decks for swift action. This would seem to describe the typical Western, which of course is pure melodrama. But many apparently more sophisticated plays, especially in films, are just as clear instances of the type: the surgeon performing a miraculous operation under handicaps, the underdog lawyer spellbinding the jury and saving the innocent defendant—these, and the scores of situations like them, insofar as the exciting action predominates over character and thought, are melodramatic. They are gripping, but they say nothing, and after we witness them we forget them.

Farce is related to comedy as melodrama is to tragedy. Farce is concerned with the ludicrous, the preposterous, with ridiculous misunderstandings and mix-ups, to say nothing of pie throwing and many other forms of horseplay, which the movies used to bill as "comedy." In farce, character counts for next to nothing, and motive is almost nonexistent; the portrayal bears a relation to life, but certainly a remote one.

It would be foolish to belittle farce and melodrama, or even to argue that they are inferior to comedy and tragedy. They are less meaningful, they are unquestionably less valuable as commentary on life, and aesthetically they are exceedingly simple. But they have their own value and make their own appeal. Perhaps we should remember that even Shakespeare made use of farce in *Twelfth Night, The Taming of the Shrew,* and elsewhere, and that *Hamlet,* for all its philosophy, superb characterization, and immortal poetry, contains a strong dash of melodrama. The point is this: we need to know what it is we are witnessing and we must value it accordingly. To put it another way, we can say that there is nothing wrong with enjoying melodrama and farce, provided we know it is these we are enjoying. The one great error we can make—and it is a most serious one—is to believe melodrama to be an honest reading of life. Of course it is not. Once we see it for what it is, however, we may enjoy it on its own terms.

THE DRAMA AND THE THEATER

The drama is unique among the major forms of imaginative literature in that it is written to be produced. The text of the play is all-important, but before it can fully realize the intention of the playwright it must be turned into a performance. Consequently we cannot ignore matters of production. Particularly in reading older plays do we need to know something about how they were produced in their time. Such knowledge helps us to visualize the action as the playwright conceived it. It also helps us to understand those features of a play that were determined by conditions of production. We need to note these conditions, then, not in order to study the art of the theater, but simply to enable us to read the plays intelligently.

If we know something of the religious origin of Greek tragedy, for instance, we can better understand the ritualistic singing and dancing of the chorus in the plays. We can also understand why the Greeks avoided violence on the stage; murder, in a theater sacred to Dionysus, would be a desecration. If we realize that Greek audiences were familiar with the stories of the tragedies, we can better appreciate how Sophocles was able to use dramatic irony so effectively. Knowing that female roles were played by men helps explain the predominance of such strong, assertive characters as Electra, Medea, and Antigone in Greek tragedy.

Similarly, a knowledge of the Elizabethan theater, actors, and audience explains some features of the plays of the period. Actors performed on a stage that projected into the audience, who stood about it or sat in surrounding galleries. The players were therefore not in front of the audience but surrounded by it. Such an arrangement made for intimacy between actors and audience, and made the "aside" a natural device. With no curtain to be drawn, action in the play could be continuous, not chopped into act and scene, as the text suggests. Absence of scenery meant that setting would have to be indicated in the actors' speeches. When we remember that female roles were played by choir boys, with trained voices, we see how fitting are the songs in the plays, and how convincing would be the portrayal of such feminine creatures as Shakespeare's Viola (*Twelfth Night*), Rosalind (*As You Like It*), and Miranda (*The Tempest*).

We cannot here consider these matters in detail. One should realize, however, that his understanding and appreciation of the plays of any age will be greatly enhanced if he acquaints himself with the theatrical conditions to which they were adapted.

For Further Reading

Brooks, Cleanth, and Robert Heilman. *Understanding Drama*. New York: Holt, 1945.
Chambers, E. K. *Shakespeare: A Survey*. New York: Oxford, 1925. (Dramabooks)
Hamilton, Edith. *The Great Age of Greek Literature*. New York: Norton, 1942.
Millett, Fred B., and Gerald E. Bentley. *The Art of the Drama*. New York: Appleton-Century-Crofts, 1935.
Ridley, M. R. *Shakespeare's Plays: A Commentary*. New York: Dutton, 1938.

· IV ·
POETRY

THE NATURE OF POETRY

Definitions of poetry are numerous. Some of them are famous. All of them, finally, are inadequate. There would be no point, therefore, in beginning this discussion with another definition. Instead, let us suppose a common situation. A man feels depressed. Perhaps things have gone against him, he has suffered a failure of some sort, his friends are indifferent to his troubles; or perhaps he can point to no cause of his depression. In either case he is dejected, feeling that the world is a sorry place and the future bleak. Now if the man tried to write, even to an intimate friend, about how he felt, he would have a hard time. He could tell how his mood made him regard the things around him, and he might try to assign causes for his mood. But exactly how he felt, the precise quality of his feeling about himself, he could hardly express at all—unless he were something of a poet.

This does not mean that all poets express moods, but it does indicate that the language of poetry is richer, more suggestive, and more powerful than the language of prose. In a sense the same language is used in both mediums. Older poetry contains some unfamiliar words, as does older prose, but most words in poems are words we know. Also, most of the features of language that we usually consider peculiar to poetry—rhythm, figurative language, sound devices—are found in prose as well. In poetry, however, they are made to count for more. They carry more meaning. For this reason we can say that language is so used in poetry as to constitute almost a separate medium. The various ways it is used are the concern of the present chapter.

Perhaps a word should be added about one of the approaches to literature mentioned in Chapter I—the close study or analysis of the work itself. It is sometimes argued that such minute study is inappropriate to poetry and that a reader need only sit back dreamily and allow a poem to affect him. One may get something from a poem in this way, especially if he hears it read by a skillful reader. Also, many simple lyrics make an immediate appeal and really require little analysis. But with more complex poems it is somehow paradoxical to adopt a relaxed, passive attitude for the reading of what almost by definition is rich, compact, and highly charged. If word for word there is more *in* poetry than in prose, it would seem that a poem demands from the reader not less but more attentiveness than does prose.

A related objection on this score is that close study spoils a poem. Examining it minutely, it is held, is like tearing the petals from a daisy: the parts are observed but the beautiful whole is destroyed in the process. The fault with this analogy is that it does not hold up. The poem cannot be destroyed; it is still there, in all its perfection, whatever one may do with it. Of course there is a measure of justice in the objection insofar as it opposes analysis for the sake of analysis, or the noting of features of a poem as isolated, unrelated matters. The lesson here, then, is that we should make our minute observations contribute in a significant way to a comment on the poem as a whole. True, art is not science. But we should not invoke this truth to justify slovenly reading.

Let us agree, then, that a poem is a complex, a whole made up of several different yet related parts and features. The final impression the poem makes upon us is a totality, as Poe said of the story, and any over-all comment of ours ought to treat the poem as a whole. But a whole is made up of parts. The more fundamental of these components are considered in what follows.

THE ELEMENTS OF POETRY

Connotation

A word is a sound or a combination of sounds which by general consent refers to, or "means," something; what it refers to—its "referent"—is what it means. A word may be used in different senses, but for each sense the word means or refers to a particular object, idea, action, quality, and so on. Such a meaning is called the word's *denotation,* which may be thought of as its core of meaning. But often a word has more than one referent; it may suggest or call to mind many things, and these, quite as much as the denotation, are also meanings. To distinguish them from the core of meaning, we call them *connotations.* Thus, "red" denotes simply the familiar color; it connotes "blood," "revolution," "danger," "anger," and so on. The phrases "flag of the United States," "the Stars and Stripes," and "Old Glory" all have the same denotation but somewhat different connotations.

In many intellectual activities it is desirable that language be as precise as possible. The lawyer, the scientist, the philosopher strive for exactness of expression, for a one-to-one relationship between the word and its referent; exact, unambiguous denotation is required in their disciplines. Indeed, it was the imprecision of words that led some philosophers to give them up altogether in favor of a system of *symbolic logic,* in which precise symbols, as in algebra, are used instead of words.

Now the poet uses words quite differently from the way in which precisionists use them. He knows that words tend to acquire clusters of association and suggestion—from the contexts in which they are used (religious, political, commercial, literary, and so on), and from the prevailing attitude toward their referents and toward the people who customarily use them. But instead of combating this tendency of language, he welcomes it and capitalizes on it. A poet pays close attention to the connotations of his words, for he knows that the nuances of associated meanings are what he is trying to convey. They will not be found in dictionaries, but they are familiar to one who is at all attentive to language.

Manuscripts of poems often show poets experimenting with different words in an effort to get the right one—"right" usually being a matter of the proper connotation. In stanza 30 of "The Eve of St. Agnes," which describes Porphyro preparing a feast of rich, exotic food, Keats changed several words to improve their connotations. The words in brackets represent his first choice, which he replaced by the words that precede them:

> . . . he from forth the closet brought a heap
> Of candied apple, quince [fruits, sweets], and plum, and gourd;
> With jellies soother than the creamy [dairy] curd,
> And lucent syrops, tinct [smooth] with cinnamon;
> Manna and dates, in argosy [Brigantine] transferred
> From Fez; and spiced dainties, every one
> From silken [wealthy, glutted] Samarcand to cedared Lebanon.

The connotations of the substituted words contribute to the rich, sensuous effect of the stanza. Sound plays a part here, too. Indeed, sounds of words and phrases often have an evocative quality that rouses emotion. Melville, for instance, thought the connotative phrase "round the world" was highly charged: "There is much in that sound," he said, "to inspire proud feelings." It should be clear, then, that since writers are sensitive to the suggestive, associational values of their words, readers must be, too, if they are to receive the full effect of what the author writes.

Imagery

The language of poetry is suggestive, as we have seen. It is also vivid. Whether the poet is seeking to evoke a sense of physical experience, to tell a story, or to discuss ideas, attitudes, and feelings, he will usually use many words that appeal to the senses. Do words actually affect our physical senses, the several means by which we perceive the world about us—sight, hearing, taste, touch, and the like? Apparently some readers are physically affected by words, but many are not. All of us, however, have "senses of the mind," so to speak, which are analogous to our physical senses and no doubt are very closely related to them. We say we "see" something in the "mind's eye," though of course our actual eyes may be closed. Again, it is possible to run over a tune in the mind, making no actual sound at all, nor even activating the muscles of the throat; yet we say we can "hear" the tune—hear it, that is, in the mind. The same is true, though perhaps to a lesser extent, with the senses of smell, touch, and so on. The major senses are these:

> sight   (the visual sense)
> hearing   (the aural sense)
> smell   (the olfactory sense)
> taste   (the gustatory sense)
> touch   (the tactile sense)
> heat   (the thermal sense)
> motion   (the kinesthetic sense)

When we say, therefore, that a poet uses words that appeal to our senses, we mean the senses of the mind. Or, to use the customary term, we say that a word creates an *image* in our mind—"a mental representation of anything not actually present to the senses," as the dictionary defines "image." All of the images called up by a poem (as well as the words that call them up) are known as the *imagery* of the poem. Sensitivity to imagery varies from person to person, but it is a quality that can be developed.

Notice how the several senses are affected by the following passages or whole poems:

1. Cold (thermal)

> St. Agnes' Eve—ah, bitter chill it was!
> The owl, for all his feathers, was a-cold;
> The hare limp'd trembling through the frozen grass,
> And silent was the flock in woolly fold:
> Numb were the Beadsman's fingers, while he told
> His rosary, and while his frosted breath,
> Like pious incense from a censer old,
> Seem'd taking flight for heaven, without a death,
> Past the sweet Virgin's picture, while his prayer he saith.[1]

2. Sight (visual), sound (aural), and motion (kinesthetic)

> Thee for my recitative,
> Thee in the driving storm even as now, the snow, the winter-day
>   declining,
> Thee in thy panoply, thy measur'd dual throbbing and thy beat
>   convulsive,
> Thy black cylindric body, golden brass and silvery steel,

[1] From John Keats, "The Eve of St. Agnes."

Thy ponderous side-bars, parallel and connecting rods, gyrating,
  shuttling at thy sides,
Thy metrical, now swelling pant and roar, now tapering in the
  distance,
Thy great protruding head-light fix'd in front,
Thy long, pale, floating vapor-pennants, tinged with delicate
  purple,
The dense and murky clouds out-belching from thy smoke-stack,
Thy knitted frame, thy springs and valves, the tremulous twinkle
  of thy wheels,
The train of cars behind, obedient, merrily following,
Through gale or calm, now swift, now slack, yet steadily
  careering . . .[2]

3. Taste (gustatory)
See the stanza, quoted above (page 49), from "The Eve of St.
Agnes."
  4. Motion (kinesthetic)

> A route of evanescence
> With a revolving wheel;
> A resonance of emerald,
> A rush of cochineal;
> And every blossom on the bush
> Adjusts its tumbled head,—
> The mail from Tunis, probably,
> An easy morning's ride.[3]

This is a poem about a hummingbird. Notice how the phrases "with a
revolving wheel" and "adjusts its tumbled head" affect our sense of motion.
Notice, too, "a resonance [sound] of emerald [color]" and "a rush [motion] of cochineal [color]"—a mixture of images known as *synesthesia*.
  5. Sight (visual), quiet (aural), touch (tactile)

> Let us walk in the white snow
>   In a soundless space;
> With footsteps quiet and slow,
>   At a tranquil pace,
> Under veils of white lace.
>
> I shall go shod in silk,
>   And you in wool,
> White as a white cow's milk,
>   More beautiful
> Than the breast of a gull.

[2] From Walt Whitman, "To a Locomotive in Winter."
[3] "A Route of Evanescence," in *The Complete Poems of Emily Dickinson* (Boston: Little, Brown & Company, 1929).

> We shall walk through the still town
> In a windless peace;
> We shall step upon white down,
> Upon silver fleece,
> Upon softer than these.

> We shall walk in velvet shoes:
> Wherever we go
> Silence will fall like dews
> On white silence below.
> We shall walk in the snow.[4]

The foregoing imagery represents physical phenomena in the world of sense. But imagery is also used to picture abstractions—ideas and feelings. A famous image in Andrew Marvell's "To His Coy Mistress" expresses the poet's sense of the swift passage of time:

> But at my back I always hear
> Time's winged chariot hurrying near.

A feeling, normally rendered only as an abstraction, is here made vivid through a combination of images—of sight, of motion, and, perhaps the most affecting of all, of sound. What makes this multiple image possible in the first place is the poet's use of personification, a figure of speech. Time (an abstraction) is pictured as a person, driving a winged chariot. The term "imagery," therefore, applies to literal words and phrases affecting the mind's senses, and also to words and phrases used figuratively. Let us keep this in mind as we go on to consider figurative language in poetry.

Figurative Language

As noted earlier, we need to go beyond the bare denotation of a poet's words if we are to catch all the meanings he tries to convey. We can say of figurative language, also, that we must "go beyond"—in this case go beyond the plain, literal meaning of a word. But there is an all-important difference between these two matters. If we note only a word's denotation and fail to go beyond to perceive its connotations as well, we miss a great deal; but if we fail to go beyond the literal meaning of a word used figuratively—fail to see, that is, that it is used not literally but figuratively—we miss everything and totally misread the word. We said earlier that a poem is a complex, and that each of its component features helps to convey meaning. True as this is, it is also true that some features are more fundamental than others. In poems that contain a great deal of

[4] "Velvet Shoes," in *Collected Poems of Elinor Wylie* (New York: Alfred A. Knopf, Inc., copyright 1921, 1932). Reprinted by permission of the publisher.

figurative language (not all poems do) one can neglect rhythm, sound, connotation, and so on, and still get something from the poem. But he who misreads the figures of speech is almost certain to misread the poem completely. Because this matter is crucial, we must consider it in some detail.

THE NATURE AND FUNCTION OF FIGURES

Differences among the several figures of speech—simile, metaphor, personification, metonymy, synecdoche—we can note presently. First let us consider a simple metaphor. Hamlet, shocked and disillusioned, is brooding over the hasty marriage of his uncle Claudius and his mother, Queen Gertrude. He says of the world,

> 'tis an unweeded garden,
> That grows to seed; things rank and gross in nature
> Possess it merely [i.e., completely].

He is not really talking about a garden, but about the world, or, rather, the moral condition of the courtly society. But "moral condition" is an abstraction; it is unpicturable, and it affects us only intellectually, not sensuously or imaginatively, as "unweeded garden" does. Hamlet feels that the moral condition of the court resembles an unweeded garden, and so says it *is* one. He is speaking, then, of an abstract state in concrete terms; or, we can say he is speaking of what is unknown to us (the moral state) in terms of what is known (the unweeded garden). The poet uses a figure—a word or phrase which is concrete and sensuous, and which refers to something familiar in our experience—to stand for the thing, idea, feeling, or attitude he is trying to communicate.

A figure, therefore, at least in good poetry, is not a mere decorative device, a "pretty" or "fancy" way of saying something which might be better said literally. A literal statement by Hamlet—"the moral condition of the Danish court is low"—would not convey a fraction of his meaning. But note how much his metaphor suggests: "Unweeded garden" calls up a picture of a lawless, ungoverned growth of coarse plants, shooting up rapidly and promiscuously and choking out the beautiful, cultivated ones. Then if, as metaphor demands, we *transfer* these qualities to the moral situation of Claudius and Gertrude, we have a vivid sense of that loathsome situation, or Hamlet's conception of it. Our senses are affected and our emotions involved, and yet Hamlet has ostensibly spoken not of the moral condition of the court but of an unweeded garden. This is what critics have in mind when they say a poem really does not mean what it says, that is, what it *literally* says. Or, as Robert Frost has put it, "Poetry provides the one permissible way of saying one thing and meaning another." Not that metaphor is a capricious or perverse device. As our example shows, metaphor is a means of enriching communication, for it enables the poet to engage our senses and emotions and imagination, as well as our intellect.

THE ANATOMY OF FIGURES

A figure speaks of one thing (often an abstraction) in terms of something else (usually something concrete and hence sensory). Between the thing talked about and the terms used to discuss it there is always a relationship, an observable association or *similarity*. We sense this likeness instantaneously as we read, just as we do in using or hearing certain forms of slang, pungent because figurative; an attractive person is a "doll," an unattractive one is a "creep," and so on. In discussing figures in poetry, however, we not only need to see what is involved in them, but we also need to have terms with which to discuss them. The comparison stated or implied in a figure can be represented as a kind of equation, if we take the equal sign ($=$) to mean "resembles." Critics have given various names to the two members of the equation. Probably those most commonly used are *tenor* and *vehicle*, suggested by I. A. Richards and C. K. Ogden. The tenor of a metaphor is the subject the poet is basically concerned with, "tenor" denoting "gist," or "general purport," as in the phrase "the tenor of his remarks." The vehicle is the figurative subject, the terms in which the poet is "explaining" or picturing his basic subject. We can represent the matter thus:

Tenor	$=$	*Vehicle*
Often abstract		Usually concrete
Unfamiliar to the reader		Familiar to the reader
Stated or implied		Stated
Example: the low moral condition of the Danish court		"an unweeded garden"

"Tenor" and "vehicle," then, are terms enabling us to discuss figures. But there is no particular value in merely giving names to the two parts of the equation; what is more important is that we observe how the poet treats them. We must, of course, allow the vehicle to make its full impression, cooperating with the poet by perceiving all the implications suggested by the vehicle. We need also to notice how he handles the tenor. The matter can be complicated, but it is possible to distinguish three main procedures. In each of the following cases the vehicle is in italics, and the tenor (when it is stated) is in boldface type.

1. The tenor may be stated separately. This occurs in all simple similes, "like" or "as" making the comparison explicit. Shakespeare's Hotspur (*Henry IV Part I*) describes a dandified messenger:

> Came there a certain **lord,** neat, and trimly dressed,
> Fresh as a *bridegroom;* and his **chin** new reaped
> Showed like a *stubble-land* at harvest-home;
> He was perfumed like a *milliner* . . . .

Another instance: Shakespeare's Sonnet 60 begins,

> Like as the *waves* make towards the pebbled shore,
> So do our **minutes** hasten to their end.

Often in sonnets based on extended similes, one main part treats the vehicle and another main part the tenor.

2. The tenor may be interwoven with the statement of the vehicle. Thus in a stanza built on an extended figure, Byron in "Stanzas for Music" compares jaded, dissipated people with victims of a shipwreck:

> Then the few whose spirits float above the *wreck* of **happiness**
> Are driven o'er the *shoals* of **guilt** or *ocean* of **excess:**
> The *magnet* of their **course** is gone, or only points in vain
> The *shore* to which their shivered *sail* shall never stretch again.

"Course" in line 3 is both figurative and literal, meaning both a ship's course and the course of one's life. There is no stated tenor for "shore" or "sail" in the last line; the implied tenor of "shore" is "goals of life," and of "sail" is "will" or "desire." The implication is clear because both halves of the nautical figure have been established in the preceding lines.

3. A poet may imply the tenor, however, even without such preparation. Robert Herrick's familiar lines are an instance:

> Gather ye *rosebuds* while ye may,
> Old Time is still a-flying . . . .

"Rosebuds" is the vehicle of an implied tenor, which we could state as "the pleasures of youth," a meaning discernible from the context but also hinted in the poem's title, "To the Virgins, to Make Much of Time." The tenor is omitted, too, in "There Is a Garden in Her Face," a song of Thomas Campion's:

> There is a *garden* in her face
> Where *roses* and white *lilies* grow . . . .

The tenor of "roses" is "pink cheeks" (implied), and of "lilies" is "fair complexion" (implied); "garden" is an extravagant collective term signifying "beautiful coloration."

KINDS OF FIGURES

"Metaphor," used in a broad sense, is the general term denoting the several figures of association or similitude we have been examining. These figures have separate names commonly used in discussions of figurative language.

1. *Simile* is the most easily recognized of the figures because the resemblance of the two things compared is explicitly pointed to by the introductory word "like" or "as." Common in popular speech ("Rumor spreads like wildfire"), it is a favorite figure with poets. Sometimes the comparison is briefly put, as in "Ode to the West Wind," where Shelley compares leaves to ghosts:

> O wild West Wind, thou breath of Autumn's being,
> Thou, from whose unseen presence the leaves dead
> Are driven, like ghosts from an enchanter fleeing . . . .

Sometimes the vehicle is elaborately expanded, as in the epic similes of Homer, or in the simile that Dr. Johnson thought the best in the language, from Alexander Pope's *Essay on Criticism*. The comparison is between working to excel in the arts and climbing the Alps:

> Fired at first sight with what the Muse imparts,
> In fearless youth we tempt the heights of arts,
> While from the bounded level of our mind,
> Short views we take, nor see the lengths behind;
> But more advanced, behold with strange surprise
> New distant scenes of endless science rise!
> So pleased at first the tow'ring Alps we try,
> Mount o'er the vales, and seem to tread the sky,
> Th' eternal snows appear already past,
> And the first clouds and mountains seem the last;
> But, those attained, we tremble to survey
> The frowning labors of the lengthened way,
> Th' increasing prospect tires our wand'ring eyes,
> Hills peep o'er hills, and Alps on Alps arise!

The two things compared in a simile are usually from different categories or realms: artistic endeavor and mountain climbing, ghosts and leaves.

2. *Metaphor* in the limited sense is calling one thing by the name of another (the world is an "unweeded garden"). Since this figure omits "like" or "as," and because the tenor itself is sometimes only implied, as we have seen, metaphor is a less obvious figure than simile. For this reason it is more surprising and hence imaginatively more effective than simile. The liberty, which poets have always taken, of calling one thing by the name of another, and of asking the reader to think of one thing in terms of something quite different from it, but significantly related at one point—it is this that does so much to give poetry the electric quality that distinguishes it from prose.

3. *Personification* endows inanimate things, including abstractions, with life and personality. The philosopher is concerned with abstractions (being, knowledge, the good, beauty), and he treats them in abstract terms. The poet, too, is often concerned with abstractions, but he renders them in

a language that is sensuous and particular. One way of rendering an abstraction in sensuous terms is to picture it as a person, much as the Greeks did in creating gods who embodied impersonal forces. Love was Aphrodite, retribution was Nemesis, and so on. As in religion, so in poetry do personified abstractions seem more real and immediate than the intellectual concepts themselves.

Poets use personification with varying degrees of definiteness. Sin and Death, guarding the gates of Hell (*Paradise Lost,* Book II), are so clearly personified as to be allegorical figures. To a large extent the same is true of the evils of life—Misfortune, Despair, Sorrow, Falsehood, Poverty, and the other "ministers of human fate"—as pictured in Gray's "Ode on a Distant Prospect of Eton College." On the other hand, although in "I Like to See It Lap the Miles" Emily Dickinson endows a locomotive with life and personality (of a nonhuman creature) when she writes

> I like to see it lap the miles
> And lick the valleys up,[5]

the identification of machine and living creature is implied in "lap" and "lick." Or consider another example, from *Hamlet:*

> the native hue of resolution
> Is sicklied o'er with the pale cast of thought . . . .

Hamlet, contemplating suicide, realizes that one's resolve to kill oneself is weakened by the thought of what lies beyond life. As Shakespeare renders the idea, he personifies "resolution" and "thought." The normal complexion ("the native hue") of resolution is ruddy, suggesting health and vigor; but now it is pale ("sicklied o'er"), the complexion ("cast") associated with thought. The personification is faint, but strong enough to call up an image, which pictures the abstraction.

4. Other varieties of metaphor include *metonymy* and *synecdoche.* Metonymy names an attribute or quality or other associated idea of a thing instead of the thing itself. In "Ode," Henry Timrod wrote:

> There is no holier spot of ground
> Than where defeated valor lies,
> By mourning beauty crowned!

Here "valor" and "beauty" name qualities of, and hence are made to stand for, fallen soldiers and mourning women. Synecdoche names the part for the whole ("crowned heads" means "monarchs"; "hands," in one sense, means "laborers"); or it names the whole for the part ("Washington reports" means "government officials in Washington report").

---

[5] In *The Complete Poems of Emily Dickinson* (Boston: Little, Brown & Company, 1929).

Of course, merely recognizing figures of speech and applying the proper names to them are of no significance in themselves, any more than the ability to spot nouns and adjectives. We do need to recognize them, but then we need to go on and evaluate them, particularly their relation to the poem in which they appear. Let us consider, then, what makes some figures more effective than others.

EFFECTIVENESS OF FIGURES

Good figures are likely to have some or all of these qualities:

1. They are *apt*. We must feel not only that the comparison is a just one, but that the vehicle really explains or sheds light on the tenor. In "A Psalm of Life" Longfellow, urging us so to live as to encourage those who come after us, expresses the idea in a metaphor. We can

> leave behind us
> Footprints on the sands of time,

footprints which may be seen by a "shipwrecked brother," whom they may cause to "take heart again." The trouble is that footprints on wet sand (and it must be wet, if they are to be seen at all) are anything but permanent. Longfellow himself recognized this fact in a later poem, "The Tide Rises, the Tide Falls," when he wrote

> The little waves, with their soft, white hands,
> Efface the footprints in the sands . . . .

Shakespeare's "unweeded garden," by contrast, is a most apt comparison. Like all good figures, it will bear the pressure of analysis; the more one thinks about it, the more illuminating it becomes.

2. Good figures are *fresh*. Indeed, they usually surprise us. Our reaction, if spelled out, is, "I never thought of these two things [tenor and vehicle] as resembling each other, but I see now that they do." The metaphysical poets of the early seventeenth century and many modern poets value surprise in their figures. They achieve it by drawing the vehicle from a realm seemingly quite remote from that of the tenor. When a close resemblance is shown to exist at one or more points in spite of the general distance between the two items, the effect is one of surprise. George Herbert wrote of God's bestowing many blessings on man when He created him, but withholding "rest," or self-satisfaction; consequently man suffers a "weariness" which draws him toward God. The poet thinks of the weariness as God's "Pulley," which is the title of the poem. The American colonial poet Edward Taylor describes the process of Christian salvation (tenor) in terms of the homely processes of spinning thread and weaving cloth (vehicle)—two realms quite remote from each other, as Professor Wallace C. Brown observed when he said that the poet was "domesticating the infinite." It is this imaginative distance between tenor and vehicle that

Emerson valued in poetry: "The meaner the type by which a law is expressed, the more pungent it is, and the more lasting in the memories of men."

3. Good figures seem *natural*. This is a difficult quality to define, but one we appreciate in a good poet. Figures in an inferior poem give the impression that the poet labored to "work them in," whereas in a good poem they have a kind of inevitability. It may be that even the good poet has to search for figures, but usually his is a mind that thinks figuratively. At least he succeeds in creating the impression that his figures were called forth by the subject and not superimposed on the poem from a misguided sense of poetic obligation.

4. Good figures are *appropriate* to the whole poem. From time to time we have said that no literary feature—word, sentence, literary device, or technique—is good or bad in itself, but only in relation to its total context. The same is true of figures of speech. A bold, metaphysical figure would be out of place in a poem of haunting atmosphere or of a marked musical quality. Sometimes, too, the tone of a poem will shift, in which case a figure appropriate in one part of the poem would not be appropriate in another. We need to ask not simply, "Is the figure good?" but, "Is it good in this poem and at this place in the poem?"

Rhythm

When we utter the sounds of human speech, they do not come out in a steady stream but rather with great variety—of stress or volume, of pitch, and of time of utterance. This variation, or pulsation, we call *rhythm*. All discourse is rhythmical, prose as well as verse, but the rhythm of verse (variation in the stress or loudness of syllables) tends to be *regular;* that is, the variations recur in a regular pattern, which we call the *meter* of the verse. As we hear verse read, or even when we read it silently, we feel the regular rhythm, much as we feel the rhythm of music. It is important that we feel it, since it contributes so much to the total effect of a poem. It is also important, however, that we analyze the rhythm, for analysis can often reveal how a poet uses rhythm to convey meaning. Although the matter is too complicated for thorough treatment here, we shall have made a good start toward understanding rhythm in poetry if we learn how to determine (1) the prevailing meter of a poem, and (2) the significant variations in the meter and the advantages of such variations.

DETERMINING THE PREVAILING METER

This is a two-step process: (1) first we discover the *kind* of feet in a line, and (2) then we count the *number* of feet in the line; these two facts constitute the prevailing meter.

1. A *foot* is the metrical unit in a line of verse. It is composed of two or more stressed or unstressed syllables arranged in one of several orders.

In reading a line of verse we lay more stress on some syllables (that is, we sound them louder and more distinctly) than on others, for one of two reasons: the normal pronunciation of a word requires it, or the sense of the line requires it. The syllables of individual words in English are stressed according to the accepted pronunciation; so, with the use of symbols, we can indicate the stress of common words: above, today, pulley, terror, interval, beautiful, overturn, underrate, jackknife, sidewalk, and so on. This is simply a matter of *word accent,* which presents no problem if we know the proper pronunciation of the word. According to another principle, that of *rhetorical accent,* we tend to stress those words in a sentence which carry the meaning—usually the nouns, verbs, adjectives, and adverbs (the content words) rather than the articles, prepositions, and conjunctions (the structural words). For example, in the first line from a Milton sonnet

> When I consider how my light is spent

we can immediately mark "consider" according to word accent (con-sid-er). According to rhetorical accent we would mark stresses for the content words "light" and "spent"; also, the sense of the line would require stress on "how." We then have

> When I consider how my light is spent.

Filling in the rest of the accents is simple in this case. Once we do it, we notice that the repeated unit of stressed and unstressed syllables—the foot—is composed of an unaccented syllable followed by an accented one (such a foot is called an *iamb*), and we separate the several units:

> When I | consid|er how | my light | is spent.

The names of the common types of feet are as follows:

Arrangement of stresses	Name	Adjectival form	Example
× /	iamb	iambic	alone
× × /	anapest	anapestic	overturn
/ ×	trochee	trochaic	harbor
/ × ×	dactyl	dactylic	terrible
/ /	spondee	spondaic	sidewalk
× ×	pyrrhic	pyrrhic	(cannot be illustrated by a single word)

2. The second step in determining the meter is simply to count the number of feet and apply the appropriate Greek term:

a line of ... is

1 foot	monometer (mo-nóm-e-ter)
2 feet	dimeter (dím-e-ter)
3 feet	trimeter (trím-e-ter)
4 feet	tetrameter (te-trám-e-ter)
5 feet	pentameter (pen-tám-e-ter)
6 feet	hexameter (hex-ám-e-ter)
7 feet	heptameter (hep-tám-e-ter)
8 feet	octameter (oc-tám-e-ter)

Since the line cited above is composed of "iambs," it is an iambic line; since it contains five of them, it is pentameter. Thus the meter of the line is said to be *iambic pentameter*. Incidentally, when scanning (that is, placing stresses in order to determine the meter), it is a good idea to work on more than one line. Because poets often introduce substitute feet, as we shall see, any given line may be irregular, and so should be checked against others.

NOTING VARIATIONS IN THE METRICAL PATTERN

Knowing the name of the meter of a poem is of little value in itself. It is, however, a necessary preparation for studying what the poet does with meter. Probably the most rewarding thing to notice is how from time to time he departs from the established rhythm. As we have seen, the poet establishes a prevailing meter, which we feel strongly as we read. But he does not feel obliged to force all his words into the established pattern; usually he departs from the pattern now and then by inserting substitute feet. For example, the prevailing meter of Shakespeare's sonnets is iambic pentameter, but notice the departures from that meter in the opening lines of Sonnet 29:

> When in disgrace with Fortune and men's eyes,
> I all alone beweep my outcast state
> And trouble deaf heaven with my bootless cries . . . .

The second line is regularly iambic, except for "outcast," the second syllable of which demands considerable stress. In scanning the line, one could give "-cast" equal emphasis with "state," making the last foot a spondee, or he could give "-cast" a *secondary accent* ('), as the dictionary does. We should recognize, of course, that any system of scansion, or marking syllables to show stress, is a crude device at best; variations in stress as one reads a line flexibly and with expression are too great to be represented by only two, or even three, different marks.

The first and the third lines of the above example are even more varied than the second. The three could be scanned like this:

/ ×　　× /　　　× 　/ × × 　　/ 　/
When in | disgrace | with For|tune and | men's eyes,

× / 　× /　　× /　　× /　 '　/
I all | alone | beweep | my out|cast state,

× 　/ × 　/　　/ ×　　× × / 　× /
And trou|ble deaf | heaven | with my boot|less cries . . . .

Technically, we would say of line 1 that a trochee is substituted for an iamb in the first foot; a pyrrhic foot for an iamb in the fourth foot; and a spondee for an iamb in the fifth foot. In the third line a trochee is substituted for an iamb in the third foot, and an anapest for an iamb in the fourth foot. We scan the line, then, according to the demands of *word accent* ("disgrace," "beweep," "trouble," and so on) and of *rhetorical accent* (giving less stress to "in," "and," "my," and so on, as a natural reading requires).

1. But although we read the substitute feet as marked, and so depart from the prevailing iambic meter, we *feel* that meter even as we depart from it. And a tension is set up at certain points between what we expect and what we get, a tension that is *interesting* and *pleasurable*. The pleasure is much like what we experience when we hear a good jazz drummer. First he establishes a good solid beat, which we feel in the blood and respond to by tapping our feet or fingers; then he departs from the beat in a variety of ways, but always, after several excursions in syncopation, he returns to the regular beat in a way that is pleasant and satisfying.

Rhythm in poetry operates in much the same way. The poet does not force his words into a metrical strait jacket, nor should we read them with barrel-organ regularity. One of the great beauties of poetry lies in the subtle modulations of rhythm effected within a framework of a definite, regular meter.

2. By using substitute feet, then, the poet can achieve a pleasing variety. But variation for its own sake, desirable as it is, is not all he can achieve. A substitute foot can also make rhythm *echo meaning*. A line from Emerson's "Merlin," which describes the ideal poet, says that "the kingly bard"

× 　　/ 　× 　　/　　/ ×　　× 　/
Must smite | the chords | rudely | and hard.

Here the sense of rudeness or roughness denoted by "rudely" is reinforced by substitution (in a way, a "rough" procedure) of a trochee for the expected iamb in the third foot. For another example of the use of substitute feet to reinforce meaning, see the quotation from Pope under "Simile."

3. Substitute feet can also *emphasize key words* in a line. Look back at the quotation from Shakespeare's Sonnet 29. The first part of the poem treats the poet's depressed state: he has had bad luck and says he is scorned or rejected by his fellows. In his dejection, he says, I "trouble deaf heaven with my bootless cries," that is, he implores the powers that be to help him, but they do not help because, being "deaf," they do not hear him. His petition to heaven shows the extremity of his depression, which is aggravated further by heaven's failure to hear his plea. He even sounds somewhat indignant and desperate at heaven's indifference to his plight. "Deaf heaven," therefore, is an important phrase in the line; in fact, it is one of the most important in the first eight lines of the poem. The substitute foot—trochee for iamb in the third foot—forces our attention on "deaf heaven," by bringing two heavy accents together. Emphasis is achieved, too, by the matching short "e" sound in "de*af* he*aven*"—a device of sound, to be considered in a moment.

To repeat, naming the meter is a preliminary step in analyzing rhythm in poetry. From there one should go on to notice how the rhythm is varied and what exactly is gained for the poem by the variation.

Sound

Poetry makes its communication with the mind, but it does so through a medium that is musical. The language of poetry is rhythmical, as we have seen; it is also composed of remarkably numerous and varied sounds, best heard when poetry is read aloud, but heard even by the "mind's ear." Sometimes these sounds create a music that is beautiful in and of itself—a pleasant accompaniment to the meanings of the words. In the best poetry, however, sound not only accompanies sense, but also helps to convey it. Let us note some of the ways it does this.

REPEATED SOUNDS

Although the term "repeated sounds" in poetry naturally suggests *rhyme* (the matching of sounds of the ends of words, particularly at the ends of lines), poetry uses matching sounds of several kinds:

Alliteration. The repetition of consonant sounds at the beginning of words or of stressed syllables:

> When I do Count the Clock that Tells the Time . . . .

(NOTE: Alliteration is a matter of the ear, not the eye; the "th" of "that" and "the" would not be said to alliterate with "tells" and "time." Neither would the "th's" in these words be said to alliterate with each other, since the words are insignificant and receive no stress.)

Assonance. The repetition of internal vowels:

> Then the mortal cOldness of the sOUl
> like dEAth itsElf comes down:
> It cannot fEEl for others' wOEs, it
> dare not drEAm its Own.

(NOTE: As with alliteration, it is the sound and not the spelling that counts; the vowel sound of "woes" is identical with that of "own.")

Rhyme. The repetition of final sounds of words, particularly words appearing at the ends of lines:

> That time of year thou mayst in me behOLD
> When yellow leaves, or none, or few, do hANG
> Upon those boughs which shake against the cOLD,
> Bare ruined choirs, where late the sweet birds sANG.

(NOTE: The above lines illustrate *exact* end-rhyme. Some poets have been fond of *approximate* rhyme: (*a*) *imperfect rhyme* [us-dust; gained-spade]; (*b*) *vowel rhyme* [be-die; me-say]; (*c*) *suspended rhyme* [near-hair; star-door].)

When sounds are repeated in these ways the effect is pleasurable. In a poem using a regular pattern of end-rhyme, the reader is constantly curious as to what word will appear to complete the rhyme; he anticipates the need for the word of matching sound, and when it appears he recognizes it as fitting. It is our satisfaction in recognizing the matching sound, plus our surprise at the word that bears it, that is the source of much of our enjoyment in poets who play with rhyme, such as Byron, Lowell, and Ogden Nash.

The patterning of end-rhymes is part of the architecture of a poem, as we shall see presently. Alliteration and assonance also have a structural function, in that *through sound* they can link key words that should be associated in the reader's consciousness. Refer, for illustration, to the quotation above under "Assonance." The relation of "coldness" and "soul" is reinforced by the matching "o" sound; and the syntactical parallelism of the two clauses in the following line is emphasized by the pairing of vowel sounds (assonance) in both "feel" and "dream," and "woes" and "own."

SUGGESTIVE SOUND

In several ways the sounds of words, besides pleasing the ear, can help to convey meaning. The clearest instance of this is the figure of sound known as *onomatopoeia,* which refers to a word whose sound resembles the thing or action denoted by the word: *buzz, toll* (of bells), *jangle, rustling, bubbling,* and so on.

This is an obvious device of sound, effective if not overdone. More subtle effects are achieved through manipulation of vowels and consonants. The long, open vowels, pronounced deep in the throat (uh, oh, ah, oo), seem more somber and grave than the short, front vowels, pronounced near the front of the mouth (i, ee, ay). No doubt this is partly a matter of individual feeling. Most attentive readers, though, would sense the change in *tone-color* (a general term denoting effects achieved by arrangement of sounds) in Shakespeare's Sonnet 29. The shift comes in line 10, where the poet, having spoken of his depressed state, says

> Haply I think on thee, and then my state,
> Like to the lark at break of day arising
> From sullen earth, sings hymns at heaven's gate . . . .

Several features contribute to the effect of joyousness: the succession of "k's" in line 2; the "run-on" line that leads us to read "arising From sullen earth" as a continuous, uninterrupted phrase; and the predominance of front vowels, as in "sings hymns," which contrasts with the back vowel of "sullen."

Or consider a phrase from Emerson's poem "The Snow-Storm," which begins by showing the effect of the storm on people about the farm:

> The sled and traveller stopped . . . .

It so happens that the first four words are composed of vowels and of consonants that either are voiced or are continuants, so that there is no interruption in the pronunciation of the line until one gets to the "pt" sound at the end of "stopped." To be sure, the words *mean* that the sled and traveler stopped; but the vowels and consonants are so arranged that the *sounds* of the words tend to convey the same meaning.

In good poetry, then, as Alexander Pope put it in his *Essay on Criticism,* "the sound must seem an echo to the sense." He illustrated the principle in the following well-known passage:

> True ease in writing comes from art, not chance,
> As those move easiest who have learn'd to dance.
> 'T is not enough no harshness gives offence,
> The sound must seem an echo to the sense:
> Soft is the strain when Zephyr gently blows,
> And the smooth stream in smoother numbers flows;
> But when loud surges lash the sounding shore,
> The hoarse, rough verse should like the torrent roar:
> When Ajax strives some rock's vast weight to throw,
> The line too labors, and the words move slow;
> Not so, when swift Camilla scours the plain,
> Flies o'er th' unbending corn, and skims along the main.

Something of a tour de force, the passage is worth study as showing what a poet can do to marry sound to sense. Rhythm, too, is here adapted to meaning. It is worth noting, finally, if one is inclined to think such effects are "accidental"—or worse, figments of the reader's imagination—that Pope is unmistakably clear in implying that the poet does these things deliberately.

Structure in Poems

In reading a poem one does not, of course, look only at the several technical features we have been discussing. What of the poem as a whole? What of the over-all statement it makes? In a sense it is true that the poem's meaning is the sum total of everything in it, which includes the ways it uses sound, rhythm, imagery, and so on. Or we can say that a poem has a core of more or less translatable meaning, to which the various technical elements contribute—their contribution often "making" the poem, that is, giving it its distinction as poetry. It will not do to equate the poem with this core of meaning, or to regard a paraphrase as the equivalent of the poem itself. Still, the core of meaning—theme, motif, idea, story, over-all feeling—does exist in the poem and, of course, is an important aspect of it. In reading a poem we should recognize this central element, and we should notice how it is composed—that is, what its parts are—for the arrangement of its parts is one of the things that gives structure to the poem.

What are the *parts* of a poem—not the formal divisions of line, stanza, and so on, which we will turn to in a moment—but the components of the central meaning or *content* of the poem? Of the many different bases of division of whole into parts, we can mention a few in order to show the kind of thing one looks for in determining the parts of the content. For instance, if the poem is a narrative, the several stages in the story are parts—parts of the plot, noted in our discussion of fiction. Even a philosophical poem may string ideas on a narrative thread, as does Wordsworth's "Tintern Abbey." In other types of poems the parts may be an aggregation of items, all of which develop a central idea: the joys of pastoral life in Marlowe's lyric "The Passionate Shepherd to His Love"; or arguments for continued endeavor in Tennyson's dramatic monologue "Ulysses." The parts may be contrasting items, as are the two different moods presented in Shakespeare's Sonnet 29 (quoted in part above) or as is the shift from grief to assurance in such elegies as Milton's "Lycidas" or Shelley's "Adonais." Some poems detail a conflict—warring attitudes or feelings—which at the end may be resolved. Whatever the terms in which the divisions may be stated, we need to discover the nature of the parts, and see how each contributes to the development of the whole central meaning.

This structural pattern of content is not always immediately apparent as we read a poem. Usually we have to think about the matter—determine the over-all meaning and then find the parts into which its development is divided. More readily seen are the several *formal* structural features of the poem: the section (book, canto, and so on), the line, and the grouping of lines in stanzas. This grouping is made according to conventional patterning of end-rhymes known as *rhyme schemes;* each new sound at the end of a line in a stanza is designated by a new letter, *a, b, c,* and so on, as in the poem quoted below.

More often than not, these formal structural divisions that strike the eye and sound in the ear will correspond to some of the real but less apparent divisions of content. In such cases the apparent form is adapted to the content and helps to shape it. A well-known instance is Shakespeare's Sonnet 73:

That time of year thou mayst in me behold	*a*
When yellow leaves, or none, or few, do hang	*b*
Upon those boughs which shake against the cold,	*a*
Bare ruin'd choirs, where late the sweet birds sang.	*b*
In me thou see'st the twilight of such day	*c*
As after sunset fadeth in the west;	*d*
Which by and by black night doth take away,	*c*
Death's second self, that seals up all in rest.	*d*
In me thou see'st the glowing of such fire,	*e*
That on the ashes of his youth doth lie,	*f*
As the death-bed whereon it must expire,	*e*
Consumed with that which it was nourish'd by.	*f*
This thou perceivest, which makes thy love more strong	*g*
To love that well, which thou must leave ere long.	*g*

The central meaning of lines 1–12 is "You see I am growing old." It is stated figuratively through three images: fall of the year, twilight of the day, and a dying fire. This pattern of imagery corresponds to the formal structure marked by the rhyme scheme, the three images being treated in the groups of lines rhyming, respectively, *abab, cdcd, efef.* In this sonnet, then, the formal pattern and the pattern of content are fitted to each other exactly. In other poems the two patterns may correspond less exactly, though with similar effect.

We have considered several technical elements one by one, and have illustrated them by excerpts from poems. It may be useful, finally, to see them exhibited in a single poem. Because Emerson's "Concord Hymn" was composed for public delivery, it expresses common emotions and makes its statement in a clear, straightforward way. It does these things artfully, however, and with some subtlety. Study it with respect to the elements discussed in this chapter. Then read Chapter VI, Assignment III, to see how one student wove his observations on these several matters into a coherent commentary on the poem.

CONCORD HYMN

Sung at the Completion of the Battle Monument,
July 4, 1837

By the rude bridge that arched the flood,
  Their flag to April's breeze unfurled,
Here once the embattled farmers stood
And fired the shot heard round the world.

The foe long since in silence slept;
  Alike the conqueror silent sleeps;
And Time the ruined bridge has swept
  Down the dark stream which seaward creeps.

On this green bank, by this soft stream,
  We set to-day a votive stone;
That memory may their deed redeem,
  When, like our sires, our sons are gone.

Spirit, that made those heroes dare
  To die, and leave their children free,
Bid Time and Nature gently spare
  The shaft we raise to them and thee.

Conclusion

Here at the end of our consideration of the three main types of imaginative literature one final word should be said. Aldous Huxley, after analyzing the prose style of his grandfather, the scientist Thomas Henry Huxley, concludes his study with this comment:

I have constantly spoken, in the course of these analyses, of "literary devices." The phrase is a rather unfortunate one; for it is liable to call up in the hearer's mind a picture of someone laboriously practicing a mixture of card-sharping and cookery. The words make us visualize the man of letters turning over the pages of some literary Mrs. Beeton in quest of the best recipe for an epigram or a dirge; or else as a trickster preparing for his game with the reader by carefully marking the cards. But in point of fact the man of letters does most of his work not by calculation, not by the application of formulas, but by aesthetic intuition. He has something to say, and he sets it down in the words which he finds most satisfying aesthetically. After the event comes the critic, who discovers that he was using a certain kind of literary device, which can be classified in its proper chapter of the cookery-book. The process is largely irreversible.[6]

[6] From Aldous Huxley, "T. H. Huxley as a Literary Man," in *The Olive Tree* (New York: Harper & Brothers, 1937). Reprinted by permission of the publisher.

In the preceding chapters we, too, have spoken of literary "devices" and "elements," which we have isolated and arranged in neat outlines. As students of literature, not writers, we are critics, who come "after the event" of literature; and we therefore are entitled, as Huxley says, to classify each device or element "in its proper chapter of the cookery-book." But of course criticism is not so mechanical as this phrase—or our outline—would seem to imply. We need to study literature in terms of its elements, but in our final critical commentary we will use them freely and flexibly. They will not be ends in themselves, but ways of allowing us to describe the nature of a literary work and to account for the appeal it makes to our minds and hearts.

For Further Reading

Blair, Walter, and W. K. Chandler. *Approaches to Poetry*. 2nd ed. New York: Appleton-Century-Crofts, 1953.

Rosenthal, M. L., and A. J. M. Smith. *Exploring Poetry*. New York: Macmillan, 1955.

Stauffer, Donald. *The Nature of Poetry*. New York: Norton, 1946.

Van Doren, Mark. *Introduction to Poetry*. New York: Dryden, 1951.

PART TWO

• V •
MECHANICS OF STUDY

This chapter suggests definite ways to go about studying literature. There is no one *best* way to proceed; you will discover a way that is best for you. But often this is a process of trial and error, which takes time and so postpones the day when you study efficiently. Following the suggestions outlined below ought to save some of that time.

KNOWING YOUR COURSE

An obvious first step is to make sure you understand the scope and method of the course you are in. As Chapter I makes clear, literature may be approached in different ways. Unless you know clearly and definitely the approach your teacher takes, you may find yourself studying the wrong thing. Ideally you should learn everything about the work you study; it would be abominable advice to urge you to pay attention only to those things that you will be held for on tests. Still, assignments are long, one has only so much time, first things must come first, and so on. It is only prudent to spend your time on matters that count *in your particular course*.

Usually your teacher will state his approach in the first session of the class—a time, unfortunately, when you are not best equipped to grasp fully what he means. He may repeat his aims later, perhaps before tests. A more reliable index of his intentions is what he does from day to day in class—the topics he considers, the questions he asks. Of course you should not assume that what occupies class time is the only thing you will be held for. One teacher may spend the hour expounding the text, relying on you to work up "backgrounds"; another may not discuss the assigned text, but lecture on historical or critical matters so as to help you read the text properly. Whatever your teacher's method, you should discover it, and so learn what he expects from you. The clearer your knowledge of this, the more efficiently can you study.

READING WITH A PLAN

It would seem that the normal way to study a work is simply to sit down and read it. Most works, however, demand more than a single reading. Ideally, the procedure is a three-stage approach: preparing to study the work, studying it, and thinking it over.

1. *Gaining a First View.* Before studying a work closely, learn something about it—who wrote it and when, what it is "about," and what literary type it is. You can gain such orientation from your textbook, from literary histories, or from published outlines. But except for such long works as novels, the best procedure is to read the work rapidly in order to get an over-all view of it. Much will escape you, but you will gain some idea of the kind of work it is and so will be ready to study it.

2. *Reading Closely.* Having a general notion of the work, you are ready to study it in detail. This involves asking questions about it, some of which are suggested below. It also involves reading with a pencil. One does not mark library books, but your own text is a different matter. Judicious marking of your textbook helps you in several ways. It forces you to read actively. If you know you must make a marginal comment on a passage, you cannot afford to read it casually and pass on. Writing something in the margin keeps you alert, and it forces you to put ideas—yours or the author's, or both—into words. Marking the text helps you to recite in class. It also helps greatly in review. Because in reviewing you cannot reread your entire textbook, it will help if you have marked your text intelligently. Then you can quickly recapture much of the exact information you had when you studied the work.

There are several kinds of things to mark in your text:

a. MARK OFF THE PARTS OF THE WORK. Determining the parts, naming and justifying them, and accounting for their order will tell you a good deal about the structure of the work as a whole.

b. UNDERLINE KEY STATEMENTS. These are statements which contain the gist of a passage, or which are notable for their expression.

c. WRITE COMMENTS IN THE MARGINS. These would include summaries of action in a narrative, character traits revealed by speech or action, paraphrases of passages (i.e., putting the author's statements in your own words), abstracts of arguments, and so on.

d. DEVELOP A SYSTEM FOR NOTING STYLISTIC MATTERS. Use different markings for different features of style. For careful work of this kind, pencils with different colored leads are useful.

In class your teacher will probably emphasize and interpret certain passages, and these you will want to mark also, if you have overlooked them in your study. Noting the differences between what you mark as significant and what your teacher emphasizes—differences that may well lead to class discussion—is an excellent way to learn.

3. *Thinking It Over.* Once you have read the work closely, there remain several things to do to make your study thorough.

a. CONSIDER THE WORK AS A WHOLE. As you read you are necessarily concerned with particular parts of the work—a scene in a novel, a soliloquy in a play, a passage in a poem. But every work should be seen as a totality, and naturally you can so see it only after you finish reading. In reading *Henry IV Part I,* for instance, you will be aware that Hotspur speaks of "honor," and you will probably notice that Falstaff also mentions it. But you will not want to pause to study closely the difference between the two opinions. This is the kind of thing you do later, when you consider the work in its larger aspects; you do it by searching the text to find all the speeches and actions of Hotspur, Falstaff, and Prince Hal that reveal their opinions about honor. You will want to ask, too, how important the theme of honor is in the play. Is it an incidental matter, or is it the core of the play's meaning—what the play is really "about"? Considering large questions like this, which often appear on examinations, is a part of "thinking over" the work as a whole, after you have studied its parts.

b. SEE THE WORK IN ITS RELATIONSHIPS. In elementary study you will be doing well if you see the work clearly by itself. Insofar as possible, though, you ought to see beyond the work to several related matters. (See Chapter I.)

(1) Relate the work to the time and place in which it was written. How are ideas of that time reflected in the work? What did people of that time think of it? What did it mean to them? (2) Relate the work to the thinking of today. How relevant to today are Milton's arguments for free speech in *Areopagitica,* Jefferson's ideas on federal aid to education? (3) Relate the work to the author's other works. Do you notice similarities of idea, form, and expression? In what ways does your author's short story resemble his other stories? Wherein is it different? (4) Relate the work to other works of the same period. Does it share their qualities? Are the qualities typical of the age? In ideas or expression does Whitman resemble Carlyle, Franklin resemble Addison? (5) Relate the work to other works of similar form or content. How does a sonnet by Milton resemble and differ from one by Shakespeare? Wherein does Mark Twain's comic treatment of animals resemble Chaucer's?

Questions of this sort often turn up on examinations. You will have a distinct advantage if you have thought about some of them ahead of time.

c. OCCASIONALLY READ CRITICAL COMMENTARY. It is true there are dangers involved here. You may be tempted to accept someone else's opinion and analysis of the work instead of forming your own. Also, as a beginning student you may find it hard to determine the value of the commentary. On the other hand, if you can avoid these dangers, you may learn a good deal by reading the commentary of readers more experienced than yourself. If you have doubts about this matter, ask your teacher to recommend a book of commentary. If he wants you to read one, he will suggest a suitable title.

d. DISCUSS THE WORK WITH OTHERS. Enjoyable in itself, talking with others about literature is a good way to clarify your opinions about it. If a friend's interpretation of a work is different from yours, make him defend his opinion; you, in turn, should defend yours. Such discussions sharpen your wits, encourage you to be articulate about your literary opinions, and consequently serve as a trial run before class sessions or examinations.

SUGGESTED STUDY QUESTIONS

Throughout your schooling you have answered many questions put to you by teachers and textbooks. As you mature, however, you are expected to ask as well as answer questions. This is not always easy to do. Each situation, object, or phenomenon that faces you is different from the one before it; what worked before will not necessarily work again. More or less true in all fields, this is particularly true in literature because every piece you read is unique. In a sense, then, the questions relevant to a work are prompted by the work itself. Nevertheless, there are a few general questions, such as those that follow, which are relevant to many works.

1. *General Questions*

a. What assumptions are implicit in the work? What does the author believe about the nature of God, of man, of society, of external nature, of art? These are large questions, and the answers are often not to be found in explicit statements but "between the lines." They are assumptions about life, and must be inferred from what is said and how it is said.

b. What is the structure of the work? What are the parts, how are they ordered, and how does each contribute to the piece as a whole? Here you are concerned not only with what a passage says but also with what it does—that is, how it functions in the whole piece. You will ask, too, whether the structure, once you determine it, is well adapted to what the author is saying. Does it perhaps, in itself, help convey what he means?

c. Is the work an artistic unity? What contributes to its unity—action, character, setting, theme?

d. What is the prevailing tone of the work? Tone is the attitude the writer takes toward his material, and many tones are possible. Particularly in poetry is this an important question, together with questions that inquire how the tone is revealed to us—that is, in what features of the work it lies.

These questions should be asked of any work. Other questions we can group by literary type. Many of them touch on matters discussed in earlier chapters. If they are not clear, refer to the earlier discussions.

2. *Questions on Fiction*

a. Do the characters fall into significant groups?

b. What is the function of each character? That is, what does his presence contribute to the story?

c. What are the outstanding traits of the principal characters?

d. How do you define the principal conflict in the story?

e. What is the course of development of the conflict? Can you represent it by a diagram?

f. How does a given episode contribute to the development or resolution of the conflict?

g. Why does a character act as he does in a given situation?

h. Does the story have a discernible theme?

i. What is the significance of the title of the story? Do the names of the characters have special significance?

j. Where, and in what proportions, does the author tell the story by means of narration (of events), description (of setting), exposition (of character), and scene (dramatic rendering, with dialogue)?

k. By what method(s) is a character made known to us?

l. How does setting function in the story?

m. From what point of view is the story told? What values result from the story's being told in this way? Does the author maintain his point of view consistently?

3. *Questions on Drama*

a. Questions a–i in the preceding section apply equally to drama.

b. Where do the main divisions occur in the play—between exposition and development, development and denouement?

c. Is the action single, or are there subordinate lines of action (subplots)? Is the subplot merely a diversion, or is it related to the main plot? If related, how is it related? By action, by character relationships, by theme?

d. Can you visualize the play on a stage? Which scenes would act particularly well?

e. What features of the play result from the peculiar conditions of production and staging at the time the play was written?

4. *Questions on Poetry*

a. Can you analyze the syntax of each sentence? Because poetry uses ellipsis (omits words) and inversions (arranges words in an unusual order), an elementary but necessary step is to determine how each word functions in the sentence.

b. Can you paraphrase (state in your own words) each passage?

c. From what source(s) does the poet draw his imagery? Does the source of the imagery shed light on his meaning? Does he use a series of consistent images (drawn from one source), or does he introduce a variety of them? What senses are appealed to?

d. How effective are the figures of speech according to the criteria suggested on pages 58–59?

e. Is the meter in any way suited to the subject or tone of the poem? How regular is it? If irregular, are the deviations significant?

f. What part does sound play in the effect of the poem? Are sound devices related in a significant way to the meaning of the poem?

Raising and answering questions like these are what is involved in studying a literary work. If you formulate these and other questions, and make a serious effort to answer them, you will have definite, detailed information about the work and can discuss it, orally or in writing, in something more than vague generalities.

PREPARING FOR TESTS

A few specific things need to be said about reviewing in preparation for tests. Because in most English courses your grade will be based almost wholly on your performance on written tests, it is only sensible to stress this phase of your study. Problems of writing an examination are discussed in the following chapter. Here let us see what is involved in preparing to write.

1. *Objective vs. Essay Tests.* We need not consider the relative merits of essay tests and objective tests (true-false, matching, multiple-choice, short answer, spotting quotations, and so on). Both are used, and the only question is, Do they call for different kinds of preparation? In general they do. An objective test calls for specific information, and usually does not require you to see things in relationship. If you can learn enough detailed facts you will manage all right. But detailed information is required on essay tests as well. A common criticism of answers to essay questions is that they lack specific detail to support general statements. Essay questions call for generalization and synthesis, but these broad statements must be illustrated and proved with details. Of course in essays you can choose your own illustrations, and for this reason you probably need less detail at your fingertips than you do for an objective test. Except for this difference—a real one—you will need specific information in both kinds of tests.

2. *Reviewing by Writing.* In reviewing you will go over your text, which you will have marked well. You will also go over your class notes—expanding and clarifying them. But it is not enough merely to "go over" these items. The term implies a process of passive absorption. You can learn more effectively if you will also do some writing. The advantages are several: Writing a thing (for example, a pertinent quotation) tends to fix it in your mind. It also forces you to notice the spelling of proper

names and unfamiliar terms. Too, it enables you to list material in groups or classes, a very real aid to memory. Finally, it forces you to think of appropriate expressions with which to discuss your subject. Many of these words and phrases will come to mind later as you write the test.

You will discover the best way to arrange your material. One way is to devote at least one large sheet to each author or major work, listing in logical groupings the facts you want to remember. Also it is helpful to marshal facts about groups of works related in theme or form, noting similarities and differences. Very likely, anything that you take the trouble to dig out of your text and notes and write down on these *review sheets,* you will remember at examination time. Ideally you prepare the review sheets some time in advance. Your final chore is to learn them.

3. *Spotting Questions.* Does it pay to try to guess what questions will be asked, in order to prepare good answers? If done properly, yes. You must not risk all on your guess. But it is only good sense to prepare some topics more thoroughly than others. This is not a matter of outguessing the teacher, but simply of putting the emphasis where it belongs. Some topics are fundamental, and your teacher probably will have emphasized them. The chances are good that you will be asked to write on them. It is hardly gambling to work up such topics with special care.

· VI ·

EXAMINATIONS

SUGGESTED PROCEDURES

Reduced to lowest terms, your work in a course is a two-part affair: learning, and telling what you have learned. Everything discussed so far relates to the first, but your performance in a course depends almost entirely on how you do the second. To make the most of your study you must do all you can to write good examinations.

This is not the place to discuss the elements of good writing. In literature courses you are expected to be able to write correctly, clearly, and effectively. The form-content relationship discussed above (pages 7–8) applies quite as much to your own writing as it does to a literary work. How you say a thing is part of what you say. If you are hazy about the principles of composition, refer to your handbook, a guide nearly as indispensable as your dictionary.

Assuming you can write adequately, let us consider what else is involved in your turning in a good paper.

1. *Look Over the Entire Test at Once.* This procedure has several advantages. For one thing, it enables you to allot your time properly. Give to each question the amount of time suggested or implied, since questions are usually weighted accordingly. If you are vague about a question, waste no time on it; eloquent verbiage will impress no one. Do only what you honestly can with the question, and spend the gained time on questions you can answer. Looking over the whole examination also encourages you to jot down immediately (on the test paper or the flyleaf of the bluebook) items relating to later questions. The psychological advantage of salting down even a few dates, phrases, or quotations is considerable. Finally, a quick over-all view permits you to keep in the back of your mind questions you will have to answer later. Points about question 4 may occur to you as you are answering question 1.

2. *Interpret the Question.* Try to see what point is involved. The questions you face will probably be drawn from one of the areas of literary study discussed in Chapter I. Your first job in attacking a question is to

notice what *kind* of information is called for, and then to plan to present that kind and no other. If you are asked to treat the structure of a poem, you will not discuss the poet's life; if asked to state the major ideas, you will not say how the poem affected you.

3. *Organize Your Answer*. Several patterns of organization are available, most of them discussed in handbooks of composition. The point is this: Usually the most desirable pattern is implied in the question. Thus, if the question asks, "In what ways does so-and-so do such-and-such," your answer clearly will take the form of enumerated points. If the question reads "Compare and contrast so-and-so with such-and-such," your organization is also clearly indicated, although you will have to decide whether to use a pattern of whole-by-whole, point-by-point, or likeness-difference, your choice depending on the material and what you want to say about it. Again, if the question asks "Why?" your answer will consist of an argument—that is, a statement involving "because," which would introduce one or more reasons. In short, the form of your answer is often dictated by the nature of the question. The one notable exception is the question that says "Discuss." Such a question would seem to be less exacting than others, for it allows you to select your material and arrange it as you choose. This very freedom, though, imposes on you the responsibility of choosing a suitable procedure, and so in a way makes for a harder assignment.

4. *Develop Your Answer*. This is a troublesome matter. A student may write four or five sentences which make truthful, accurate statements; yet when his paper is returned, he finds his answer graded C. Since there are no red marks in the margin, he cannot see why the answer is not worth more. If he is told that his answer is thin, that he should have written more, he may still be confused. Isn't it desirable, he asks, to get things said as succinctly as possible? Yes, often it is, even on tests, especially when the directions call for brevity. But an essay question to which you are asked to devote twenty minutes or more calls for a well-developed answer. Sometimes students realize this, yet find it hard to know *how* to develop an answer. In an effort to fill up space they include material irrelevant to the question, or they give lengthy summaries of the piece under discussion.

The best way to see how topics can be developed is to review the matter of "paragraph development" in a good handbook of composition. Of the several methods usually listed (definition, comparison and contrast, analysis, and so on), one of the most useful is "illustration." A broad question will call forth some broad statements in the answer, but these should be supported with particulars, in order to improve the exposition and, more importantly, to show that you know the subject in some detail. Learning how to work into your discussion specific references (including apt quotations) will improve your answers considerably.

5. *Watch Matters of Style*. No one of the following items is crucial, but each is worth handling properly.

a. Set your answer up neatly, especially if you are presenting enumerations in discussion or tabular form.

b. See that your answer is self-contained. If the question reads "Why did Thoreau go to live at Walden Pond?" you would *not* begin your answer by saying "He went there because . . ." but rather "Thoreau went to live at Walden Pond because . . . " thereby incorporating the terms of the question in your opening statement.

c. Present titles correctly. Titles of works separately published (novels, plays, for example) should be underlined. Titles of parts of works (individual poems or stories appearing in a collection or a periodical) should be enclosed in quotation marks. The date of publication, if needed, should appear in parentheses immediately after the title.

d. Refer to deceased male authors by their last names. On examinations the same is usually permissible for living authors as well. In referring to a woman writer, living or dead, use "Miss" or "Mrs.," or her full name. Thus, "Miss Dickinson," or "Emily Dickinson," but not "Dickinson" or "Emily."

e. In recounting the action in a literary work, use verbs in the present tense. ("Hamlet fights with Laertes," not "fought.")

f. Avoid referring pronouns to nouns in the possessive case, as "In Thoreau's *Walden* he tells about . . . ." Rather say, "In *Walden* Thoreau tells about . . . . "

6. *Reread Your Paper.* Allow several minutes to read over your paper before you turn it in. Try to catch careless errors and to improve your expression. It is quite permissible to cross out words and insert others, even though you write in ink, as you should certainly do.

SAMPLE ANSWERS TO EXAMINATION QUESTIONS

The following student papers illustrate several matters discussed above, both in the present chapter and earlier. Most of them are answers to examination questions, which vary considerably in subject, in method, and in difficulty. They vary also in excellence, although no poor ones are included. Following each question is a brief statement of what it involves. Following each paper is a brief comment on the virtues and shortcomings of the answer.

Assignment I: Paradise Lost (Books I & II) and *An Essay on Man* (Epistle I) invite comparison, since the authors of both poems are attempting to "justify [Pope says 'vindicate'] the ways of God to men." What is meant by the phrase to "justify the ways of God to men"? Point out the most important differences between the two poems. (30 minutes)

Analysis of Assignment: The question asks the student to see two works in relationship to each other. (See 3 b(5) under "Reading with a

Plan" in Chapter V.) The reason for considering them together is stated in the question, although the student is asked to explain the common phrase that unites them. After treating this resemblance, he is asked to point out differences—an assignment calling for an enumeration, and possibly a classification, of points.

Paper A

"To justify the ways of God to men" means that Pope and Milton are trying to show us that God's plan for us is right. God's ways do need explaining because people don't understand why there is evil in the world when God has the power to stop the evil.

Although Pope and Milton have the same purpose in their compared works, there are many differences in the poems themselves. Milton tries to justify the ways of God by using a story with characters. Pope does this by a discussion using rational reasoning and philosophy. The God of Milton is all powerful, while Pope believes in Deism which accepts an impersonal God. Milton writes in blank verse using long sweeps of expression while Pope writes the heroic couplet. The world of Milton is not static. On the other hand, Pope follows Sir Isaac Newton in his belief that the world is not changing, it is fixed. Pope gives man an actual place in the chain of being, while Milton does not. Pope does not write in the supernatural or religious vein, while Milton does.

Comment: The answer is not self-contained. (See Point 5b in the first part of this chapter.) The organization is adequate. Paragraph 2 makes a point-by-point contrast. It would be improved if the nature of the points of difference, here implied, were explicitly stated. (E.g., "The two poems differ also in verse medium. *Paradise Lost* is written in blank verse . . . . Pope writes the heroic couplet.") The most notable shortcoming, since one-half hour was allowed for the question, is that the answer lacks development. (See Point 4 in the first part of this chapter.)

Paper B

Down through the ages, man has been mystified by the ways of God. He finds it hard if not impossible to comprehend why God acts as he does toward his creation. Indeed, some men even challenge the justness of these ways and wish to tell how things should be. Pope and Milton wish to clarify and show the justice of the ways of God by giving man an insight into the vastly greater perspective of the whole creation and its history. By giving man a look at the history that led up to the present state of affairs, Milton can make God's ways seem more just and clear. Pope wishes to show man that, if viewed as a whole rather than as a small part, the world is entirely just. In a word, if viewed from the correct perspective, "Whatever is, is right."

Milton uses the epic form to convey his message. He invokes a muse of wisdom to aid him to set down the story. He has the rich imagery and supernatural creatures of the epic. He conveys his meaning using the long epic simile, and the long sweeping verse paragraph. There is a vast pageant of characters, with their formal speeches and lofty, dignified language, and all the other elements of the typical epic.

Pope, on the other hand, uses a straightforward language of reason and logic. His appeal is not to the senses and emotions, but to the reason and intellect. He sets his argument down in cold clear logic—poetic and beautifully quotable, yes, but intellectual and philosophical. His "muse" is the philosopher on whom he bases his view. His imagery is of a whole creation which is like a vast, perfectly functioning machine, wherein every part serves its function and only that function. His "similes" are more likely syllogisms, which prove his point. Milton uses a story of history to bring out the point that man was once perfect and deserved only the love of God, but that now through the corruption and fall man is imperfect and needs the help of the Messiah to regain heaven.

Pope uses logical argumentation to show that man is imperfect only in the mind of men, who view the cosmos from the limited perspective of one part of a gigantic whole. Man is really quite perfect, insofar as he is a part of the creation, just in the right place in the vast system of subordination and gradation.

Pope says man brings on his misery by this wishing to be something higher than he is meant to be. He wishes to have the more perfect spirit of the Angel and also the more perfect body of the brute. Man is miserable in always trying to leave his proper place and be something else.

Milton shows that man's life was made miserable by his loss of Paradise brought on by his corruption by Satan and the fallen spirits of Hell. He is now in the miserable state of fearing death, disease and all the things which were not a part of Paradise. Only through the Messiah can he be redeemed.

Comment: The opening paragraph is good; it opens with a large general truth, narrows to a statement of the relation of Pope and Milton to this truth (here the titles of the two poems should have been mentioned), and concludes with a fairly satisfactory broad statement of the difference between the two poems. The rest of the essay contains a number of valid and significant differences, though additional detailed references to the poems would help. The chief shortcoming is in the organization; the shuttling between Pope and Milton is clumsy.

Assignment II: Write an extended critique of that portion of Chapter 31 of *Huckleberry Finn* in which Huck struggles with his conscience. Show how the author presents the struggle, and mention the values inherent in the passage. (An "open-book" question.)

Analysis of Assignment: The task here is to analyze Mark Twain's method in presenting the struggle, and to determine the values of the passage. Since "values" is plural, one should think of different *kinds* of value—social, moral, aesthetic, emotional, and so on.

Paper A

In chap. 31 of *The Adventures of Huckleberry Finn,* published in 1885, Mark Twain shows Huck wrestling with his conscience about whether he ought to send Jim back to his owner, Miss Watson. At first he thinks he should not write a letter to Miss Watson, telling her that he has Jim, and that he will bring him back. But then he gets to thinking that this is not right, because a slave is property, and one is obliged, according to the code of the day, to return runaway slaves. So in spite of his decision, he begins to realize that he is doing wrong. The reason he is doing wrong, he realizes, is that he has not been brought up right; he has never been taught what is right and what is wrong. But then his conscience tells him that this is his own fault:

> "There was the Sunday-school, you could 'a' gone to it; and if you'd 'a' done it they'd 'a' learnt you there that people that açts as I'd been acting about that nigger goes to everlasting fire."

He doesn't know what to do, and so decides he will write Miss Watson a letter and then see how he feels after he has done it. (His test of good conduct here reminds me of Ernest Hemingway, who said you know an action is good if it makes you feel good after you have done it. Hemingway may have got the idea from Mark Twain.)

But Huck doesn't feel any different after he writes the letter. In fact he begins to feel bad (though at first he feels good). But when he begins to think of all the kind things Jim has done for him, he begins to realize that it would be a cruel and heartless thing for him to turn Jim back to slavery. Here again his conscience works actively. (Possibly Mark Twain is putting something of himself in the story at this point; he, too, had a very active conscience, which troubled him often.)

He is now back where he was when he started. He decides again that he will not write the letter. In fact he tears up the letter:

"All right, then I'll go to hell"—and tore it up. Of course it is amusing to us that he should think he will go to hell for doing this, because we realize that he really is doing a good act, at least according to the way we look at the matter today, though not according to the prevailing view in the South in the days before the Civil War. Huck is acting, according to the Southern code, in a way that is wrong; and he is so indoctrinated with these ideas that he is convinced his action is a wrong one. We feel that this is amusing, although I doubt that people reading the book in 1885 would have thought so.

In Mark's earlier writing (both in *Life on the Mississippi* and in *Tom Sawyer*) he portrays a young boy troubled by an over-active conscience. In *Huckleberry Finn* he is doing the same thing, but I think he does it better here. It is a very convincing treatment of how a boy's mind works; boys are often troubled with such problems—more than adults realize—and Mark Twain has written this passage to make it realistic, just the way life is. Partly this is due to Huck's language; he talks the way a boy of his education would talk, and this helps to make it all very real and convincing. The realism, plus the humor that results from Huck's predicament and his effort to get out of it, makes the passage a good one. Also, it seems to me, that it has a good deal of satire in it, since Mark Twain is making fun of the old ideas on slavery.

Comment: The expression is casual and careless. Irrelevancies are introduced (the reference to Hemingway, to Mark Twain's life, and to his other writings). A more serious objection is that the bulk of the discussion is not analysis but a summary of the action—not a statement of how the author "presents the struggle," but a statement of what Huck does. The critical value of the last paragraph is negligible. As to values, satire is underplayed, humor overplayed.

Paper B

The episode in Chapter 31 of *Huckleberry Finn*, in which Huck debates whether to inform Miss Watson of Jim's whereabouts and so to return him to bondage, is perhaps the high point of the novel. Although not the climax in the structural sense, since it does not precipitate the resolution, the episode is rendered with great clarity and vividness, and is probably the richest passage, both morally and emotionally, in the entire book.

When "for forty dirty dollars" the King sells Jim down the river, as it were, Huck believes that Jim would be better off with Miss Watson. Should he or should he not write to her? It is a hard question, and three times he decides it, twice tentatively, once decisively. In his usual pragmatic way Huck tests each tentative decision by noting how he feels after making it. After the first decision—not to write the letter—he feels miserable; after the second, and after (again pragmatically) actually writing the letter, he at first feels good, but gradually comes to feel miserable about this decision, too. In both cases the test of his decision is conscience, which, he says, "went to grinding me." But it is a different conscience in each case. In the first it is the conscience responsive to public morality; in the second that of personal morality. Huck's first dilemma involves a conflict between his respect for convention (the accepted views on slavery) and his fear of shame (for having aided a runaway slave). The second dilemma also involves respect for convention, but opposed to it this time is fear of ingratitude—for all that Jim has done for Huck. Badgered by his "public" conscience in the first dilemma, Huck feels sinful, tries to pray, but discovers "you can't pray a lie"; convention wins out over the selfish motive—fear of shame. But it is overcome by the noble motive— Huck's vivid recollection, through the promptings of his "private" conscience, of what Jim is and what he means to him. He tears up the note, resigned and even willing to *"go* to hell." Herein lies the central irony of the passage—the boy thinking his action wrong, when by any enlightened moral standard it is thoroughly virtuous.

The complex of emotions evoked by the passage is remarkable. We feel indignation toward the society that practices slavery, particularly as it is seen to have warped the thinking of a naturally generous nature. We feel pity for Huck, both because he is the victim of society, and also because, a mere youngster, he is asked to resolve one of the most difficult of moral problems —the conflict of public as opposed to private morality. But we feel, too, a certain elation in realizing that human nature is partially redeemed by Huck's conduct. And we feel amusement in Huck's moral stumbling—a feeling which, oddly, does not clash with the others, perhaps because Huck's pragmatic method proves finally effective.

That Mark Twain could achieve all of this in the language of an "illiterate" frontier waif is an indication of his genius.

Comment: This paper meets the assignment much better. The opening paragraph economically relates the passage under discussion to the novel as a whole, and announces the organization that the discussion will follow—a two-part discussion, of analysis and evaluation. The analysis is clear, and is particularly successful in avoiding summary and in abstracting and naming the forces at work in Huck's mind. Possibly the discussion is *too* abstract here, and would have been improved by including additional specific references to Huck's actions. The evaluation, in paragraph 3, is made in terms of the reader's emotions. This paragraph implies (and might well have stated explicitly) several kinds of values in the passage.

Assignment III: Write a detailed critical analysis of Emerson's "Concord Hymn." (An assignment to be done outside class.)

Analysis of Assignment: This assignment calls for statements about individual parts and features of a work, and their relation to the work as a whole. (See 1b under "Suggested Study Questions" in Chapter V.) For the text of the poem, see the conclusion of Chapter IV.

Paper

Ralph Waldo Emerson's short commemorative poem, "Concord Hymn," stands at the gateway separating his literary career from his work in the ministry and is of interest as a marker and as an example of how occasional verse can sometimes achieve a lasting popularity despite the ephemeral nature of the motivating "occasions." This quality of immortality often attaches itself to verse which celebrates an historical incident that grows or has grown into a tradition and thereby becomes a part of a people's heritage. Such an incident is the battle which called forth Emerson's poem.

The famous fight with the redcoats had taken place almost under the shadow of Concord's manse, an Emerson family home. Grandfather Ripley, now the master of house and land, had given the town a slice of his little field on condition that the grant should be fenced with heavy stone and that a monument commemorating April 19, 1775, should be erected on the ground by July 4, 1837. The cornerstone was laid late in 1836, but the monument, though it bore that date, was not dedicated till the following Fourth of July. . . . When the original hymn by a "citizen of Concord" was read by Ripley and "beautifully sung" by a choir to the tune of Old Hundred, the author was not there to hear, being absent on a visit to Plymouth. . . . The "assembled multitude" was "highly gratified and deeply impressed" by the day's exercises and may have approved the local paper's judgment that the hymn spoke for itself and that it at once excited ideas of originality, poetic genius, and judicious adaptation. . . . The "Concord Hymn," as it was later called, was at once taken up by the newspapers, though it was some thirty-eight years before its opening lines were cut in stone on the farther side of the river. (Ralph L. Rusk, *The Life of Ralph Waldo Emerson* [New York, 1949], pp. 273–74.)

The poem is composed with a metrical regularity seldom found in Emerson's later verse. It consists of four quatrains, rhyming abab, cdcd, efef, ghgh, and is in very regular iambic tetrameter, which is varied by several trochaic and anapestic feet. The first stanza is an excellent introduction to such an occasional piece and gives both the location and the time of the event while also suggesting its nature. The second stanza introduces images of the silent dead and of the relentless passage of destructive Time. In the third stanza we are brought to the present action and are given the motivation for it: "That memory may their deed redeem." The concluding stanza begins with an apostrophe to "Spirit," the master of "Time" and "Nature." Here the hymn requests that "Spirit" bid "Time" and "Nature" to spare the monument.

The poem's movement can be regarded as a point on a fluctuating time continuum. Stanza one, with its verbs in the past tense, evokes the past. In the second stanza the past blends with the present as both past tenses ("slept" and "has swept") and present tenses ("sleeps" and "creeps") are used. The past is given the greater emphasis through references to the "foe" and the "conqueror," who are now dead. The personification, "Time," is also introduced here and is imaged as a destructive force that has literally swept the old bridge down the stream. The third stanza brings us to the action of the present and, in phrases yoked by alliteration ("our sires" and "our sons"), suggests a future. The concluding stanza now brings all times together with references to the "heroes" of the past, the "children" of the present, and the memorial "shaft" which, if the prayer be answered, will preserve the memory of the "heroes" into the future.

The four stanzas show a very tight continuity, which is made possible through the suggestive and logical links between stanzas, and through the use of parallelism. The lines "And fired the shot heard round the world" end the first stanza and suggest, in conjunction with "embattled," the warfare which resulted in the deaths of the "foe" and the "conqueror" in stanza two. Again, in the second stanza, a transition is provided by the movement of the "dark stream," here suggestive of the ravages of Time, into the "soft stream" of stanza three. The transition between stanzas three and four is less smooth. Although there is a continuation of imagery in the paralleling of "sires" and "sons" in stanza three and "heroes" and "children" in stanza four, the initial trochee in line 13 interrupts the transitional movement. The interruption is appropriate, however, since it coincides with the introduction of the apostrophe to "Spirit."

The few departures from the iambic foot seem to have little purpose other than that of providing variation, although the trochees at the beginning of the first and fourth stanzas would seem to provide the emphasis with which a singing group usually accentuates the first word of a stanza, especially in the first and last stanzas of a hymn. A certain symmetry can also be seen in the initial trochees in the last lines of the second and third stanzas, but an organic necessity for this symmetry seems improbable.

There are very few connotative words in the poem. Those which are suggestive are of that familiar nature necessary to elicit a response, conscious or unconscious, from the general public. Such words as "rude bridge," "dark stream" and "creeps" are common and are suggestive to most people. Nevertheless, such suggestive contrasts as "dark stream" and "soft stream" are quite effective and the use of the relatively unfamiliar word, "votive," seems to give the poem an elevation that would naturally impress such a gathering. Alliteration is also quite well handled and the use of s's in stanza two is very effective in the imaging of men that sleep, Time that sweeps and streams that creep.

The poem as a whole is well composed, considering the incident and the audience to whom it was addressed. In fact, it has some claim to posterity on its own merits, quite aside from the obvious appeal to the national pride and the local pride of men whose ancestors fired the "shot heard round the world." Although this latter appeal has a great deal to do with the poem's immediate and lasting popularity, the poem, as I have intimated, deserves consideration on grounds other than that of mere occasional verse.

Comment: The paper makes intelligent statements about particular features of the poem and relates these to the whole poem. It does an especially good job of seeing the poem (both as a whole and in its parts) as it is related to the time and occasion that prompted it. (See 3b under "Reading with a Plan" in Chapter V.) Although the assignment does not specifically require the student to see the poem in its historical context, the writer of the paper wisely chose to do so. Viewing the poem historically enabled him to say significant critical things about it. The paper is commendable also for its critical detachment. Making a fresh appraisal of such a familiar poem as the "Concord Hymn" is not easy. Finally, the paper is good because it succeeds in weaving together a number of separate "points" into an interesting and graceful essay.

Assignment IV: Discuss Henry James's idea of the artist's relation to society, as revealed in "The Lesson of the Master" and "The Death of the Lion." (30 minutes)

Analysis of Assignment: Assignment I involved two works by two authors. The present assignment involves two works by the same author. It differs from Assignment I also in not indicating whether the two works embody different ideas or the same idea; it is up to the student to determine this and to make clear his opinion. (See 3b(3) under "Reading with a Plan" in Chapter V.)

Paper

A fairly consistent view of the artist's relation to society is embodied in the series of stories that James wrote concerning artists, and it is reinforced in his criticism. In "The Lesson of the Master," for instance, James portrays the conflict between two kinds of passion that might roughly be termed intellectual, or artistic, and human, or social. James's point is that the satisfaction of one passion is the stultification of the other.

By finding a perfect wife, Henry St. George has become so integrated with his home and with society that his work has suffered aesthetically. He has lost both his intellectual and financial independence almost against his will. Realizing this, he takes refuge in verbal and behavioristic irony. The lesson he teaches Paul Overt—oddly enough by re-marrying—is that the two passions are incompatible, that one must choose between his art and his life. Characteristically, James reverses the traditional notion of woman as inspiration. Perhaps because of the reception of his own work, and his early physical tragedy, James is one of the first nineteenth century authors seriously to hold the isolated artist position in its anti-romantic form. In our own century, in the works of Thomas Mann, the artist will not only be isolated, but diseased.

In "The Death of the Lion," James deals with the same dichotomy between art and life; but this time it is in terms of the artist and the crowd. Neil Paraday is destroyed, on the narrative level, by the time-demands that an unknowing and barbarous crowd make upon him. Metaphorically his death as an artist results from his being "taken up" by society. Once his splendid isolation is lost, both his time and (James suggests) his ability are destroyed. James rather cleverly demonstrates the corruption of talent by society, not in Paraday himself, but in the comic characters, Guy Walsingham and Dora Forbes.

This same thesis is implicit in the essay, "The Art of Fiction"—the notion that it is the artist's own consciousness which must be protected from society. Consequently, in that essay, the reader is asked to "like" what James likes and to consider as "important" what James so considers. It is this evaluatory ability which the artist sacrifices when he becomes a part of society, for the simple reason that he no longer has distance enough to see clearly. The isolation of the artist, then, is the condition of his art. The famous "house of fiction" metaphor, in the preface to *The Portrait of a Lady*, illustrates James's views as well as any of his stories. For James, artists are *inside* a house looking out at life. They may change the size of the window (point of view), but to go out the door is aesthetic death. Once outside, they can neither see clearly nor communicate formally.

Comment: The opening sentence immediately makes clear that both stories embody the same idea; it also prepares for the introduction of the last paragraph, on James's criticism. Although in the assignment nothing was said of James's critical writings, mentioning them in the essay is quite legitimate, since they help to define James's idea; the unasked-for material is not irrelevant. The discussion of the two stories is commendably succinct, the writer avoiding tedious summary, yet indicating clearly in his general statements all that the assignment requires. The paper also demonstrates how one can derive an author's opinion from his fiction. (See pages 29–30.) "Hold," toward the end of paragraph 2, is ambiguous. Otherwise the answer is excellent.

Comments on these several essays have said nothing about the accuracy of information contained in them. Although such accuracy is obviously of great importance in any answer to an examination question, we have necessarily been concerned here with the form and method of answers. There is an art to writing good examinations. You will help yourself a great deal, practically speaking, if you do all you can to master it.

INDEX